SHIELDING OUR INNOCENTS

A PREVENTION PLAN ON CHILD SEXUAL ABUSE

HÉLÈNE HINSON STALEY

Foreword by

ROLAND C. SUMMIT, M.D.

Publisher's Cataloging-in-Publication (Provided by Quality Books, Inc.)
Staley, Hélène.
    Shielding our innocents : a prevention plan on child sexual abuse / by Hélène Staley.
    p. cm.
    Includes bibliographical references.
    Preassigned **LCCN: 97-93262**
    ISBN: 0-9657496-0-6
       1.Child sexual abuse--Prevention. 2.Adult child sexual abuse victims--Interviews. 3.Child molesters--Interviews. I. Title.
HV6570.S73 1997   364.1'536
                        QBI97-40461

Metallo House
PUBLISHERS

ACKNOWLEDGMENTS

My appreciation is extended to everyone who assisted me during the research and writing phases of *Shielding Our Innocents, A Prevention Plan On Child Sexual Abuse* -- including all interviewees named and unnamed throughout the book.

HOW TO CONTACT THE AUTHOR

You may send your comments in regard to *Shielding Our Innocents, A Prevention Plan On Child Sexual Abuse* to Hélène Staley, Post Office Box 1071, Sanford, North Carolina 27330 or by fax: (919) 774-5611.

HOW TO ORDER ADDITIONAL COPIES

Libraries and individuals may order additional copies of *Shielding Our Innocents, A Prevention Plan On Child Sexual Abuse* by writing directly to Metallo House Publishers, Post Office Box 1071, Sanford, North Carolina 27330 and sending a check or money order for $14.95 plus $3 for shipping and handling for single orders.

This book is dedicated to Scott, Chad, Chloe and every child who has ever suffered, died from or survived any sort of abuse.

Endorsement

"One woman's impassioned plea on behalf of child victims of sexual assault to waken societal awareness, understanding and action. Hélène Staley targets parents, professionals, and the media to conscientiously listen to accounts of victims and offenders, to push aside naiveté and denial, and use resources and strategies she has researched hoping to make a difference in preventing child sexual abuse."

Lisa Amaya-Jackson, M.D., M.P.H.
Director, Child & Adolescent Trauma Evaluation, Treatment &
Research Program
Duke University Medical Center
Durham, North Carolina

SHIELDING OUR INNOCENTS,

A PREVENTION PLAN ON

CHILD SEXUAL ABUSE

BY
HÉLÈNE ANDORRE HINSON STALEY

PUBLISHED BY:
METALLO HOUSE PUBLISHERS
POST OFFICE BOX 1071
SANFORD, NORTH CAROLINA 27330

PUBLISHERS

"For surely, O Lord, you bless the righteous;
you surround them with your favor as with a shield."
-- Psalm 5:12. (NIV).

Contents

Shielding Our Innocents,

A Prevention Plan

On Child Sexual Abuse

By: Hélène Andorre Hinson Staley
Foreword by: Roland C. Summit, M.D.

Dedication

Information * }

CHAPTER
2

{ * To Cope And Heal/Or Cope And Fester * Three Accounts
From Women Survivors Sexually Abused By Their Stepfathers * To
See, Listen And Learn * What We Can Do To Prevent
Opportunities For Offenders * Realities * Three Accounts From
Women Survivors Sexually Abused By Their Brothers * Notes On
Prevention * Man's Recollection Of Child Sexual Abuse By His
Teacher * Account From A Teacher -- Sexually Abused By Her
Natural Father And Her Father's Friends * Prevention Summary
And Checklist For Chapter II * Prevention Checklist * }

CHAPTER
3

{ * What Can We Learn From Offenders? * Taking A Closer Look
At Society * Appearances Can Be Deceiving * Who Do Offenders
Seek As Victims? * Portrait Of A Sex Offender * Accounts From
Sexual Offenders (In Active Therapy) * Prevention Summary
Checklist For Chapter III * Checklist * }

CHAPTER
4

Foreword
By: Roland C. Summit, M.D.

The mid-seventies of the twentieth century marked a renaissance of concern for sexually abused children. Despite a series of evanescent rediscoveries in 1850 and 1896 and 1933, the natural state of public consciousness has been deliberate ignorance. It is as if we as an adult society simply will not tolerate the pain of empathic awareness of sexually victimized children.

In 1975, there seemed to be a new threshold for enduring concern. Women were asserting their rights to protest rape and to share with one another the shame-locked secrets of their childhoods. Child battery had been rediscovered more than 10 years before. X-ray pictures of broken bones had finally been allowed to speak for children who had hidden their broken hearts with stoic silence. Surely now we could understand that legions of children could be sexually victimized without complaint. And surely we could accept from the testimonials of now-empowered women that sexual abuse could be an overwhelming, soul-shattering experience.

So it seemed in 1975. Within the next three years popular books and professional monographs exploded forth. *Kiss Daddy Goodnight. The Best Kept Secret. Conspiracy of Silence. The Common Secret. Father Daughter Incest. Sexual Abuse of Children. The Broken Taboo. Daddy's Girl.* By the end of the decade the tide was obviously at a height that would forever wash away the misfortunes of silent entrapment. These anthologies of survivor experience were compelling, irresistible. No amount of traditional denial and indifference could turn such a tide.

And yet, near the end of this century, as in an earlier *fin de siècle*, the cleansing waters of credulity are in retreat. An insistent, increasingly powerful and sophisticated skepticism has challenged almost every tenet of child protection and survivor recovery. Children are subject to *taint hearings* which may discredit their complaints as a reflection of purportedly biased investigation. Multivictim scenarioes are dismissed as products of mass hysteria and overzealous therapists. The phenomenon of traumatic amnesia and the attendant recovered memories of surviving adults are branded as categorically *False Memories* amidst lawsuits leveled at therapists who supposedly inspired false accusations.

Ironically, the shift in public sympathy from victims of sexual abuse to victims of allegations of sexual abuse has relied on the triumph of objectivity over emotion, of "*scientific studies*" over "*anecdotal evidence.*"

While it is possible to contrive laboratory experiments which induce children to falsely report benign experiences, and while adults can be tricked into "*remembering*" events that never happened, it is ethically impossible to synthesize the conditions of terror, annihilation and betrayal that could demonstrate the origins of helpless silence and traumatic amnesia. These conditions that victims, survivors and their therapists "*know*" to be real are no more real to outside skeptics than were the Sesame Street children's experience with Mr. Snuffleupagus. A quality of childlike naïveté is required to enter willingly into the ambiguities of childhood experience. That quality passes for gullibility if it leads one to listen for and to believe previously unheard complaints of sexual assault. Pretentious scientists have little tolerance for "*poorly trained clinicians*" who succumb to the emotional trap of the merely anecdotal.

Yet it is only the self-reports of sexually abusing or of being sexually abused that can illumine that dark shadow of human experience. Unless we reexamine the anecdotes and refocus our agendas of understanding we may all escape again to the traditional luxury of not knowing.

This book is about knowing. It reasserts the now-quaint appeal to understand the importance of sexual abuse by listening to voices of experience. This is a book of anecdotes and reflections. It is thoughtful, thought-provoking and moving. It is a study in the style of the recent past designed to renew our hopes for a brighter future. Like its counterparts from the mid-seventies, it comes when there is a pressing need for a reassessment of prevailing indifference.

Helene Hinson Staley is a writer with a mission. As a reporter assigned to the criminal court she saw victimized children discredited and their accused molesters set free. As an investigative reporter she sought out adult survivors of child sexual assault, as well as, convicted offenders in order to experience the emotional nuances of victimization and victimizing. As a researcher she interviewed clinicians and perused available literature to gain foundations for her views. And as an especially human being, a woman, wife and mother she brings a sanguine personal intensity to a subject lately encumbered with sopistry and stifling dissention. The result is *Shielding Our Innocents:* a book worth reading about a subject too long neglected.

Roland C. Summit, M.D.
Head Physician, Community Consultation Service
Clinical Associate Professor of Psychiatry
Harbor-UCLA Medical Center

Shielding Our Innocents,

A Prevention Plan

On Child Sexual Abuse

INTRODUCTION

"Each harmful and cruel abusive act cripples a child's potential to become a healthy, normal adult."
{ Source: A pamphlet titled: *"It shouldn't hurt to be a child,"* **by North Carolina Chapter of the National Committee to Prevent Child Abuse. * Reprinted with permission. }**

My Comments To You

Why Should You Read This Book?

Look into the innocent eyes and faces of children around you. Imagining fates of sexual abuse brings disgust to most of us, but some of us are comforted that we are only reading about victims we do not know or hearing television news reports on survivor statistics -- again people we don't know or talk to. The crime then feels less real. We find comfort in distancing ourselves from the nightmares of the innocent.

Our approach to preventing child sexual assault or abuse (I use the words *"assault"* and *"abuse"* interchangeably because they actually mean the same thing.) must be aggressive. To obtain an education about any social problem and then not use the information to prevent or solve, keeps us in the same place. Reading this book offers more than comfort for the offended and information on what to look for when it is suspected a child is being abused. It offers a personalized prevention plan, one you can formulate from the ideas presented in this book and from the lists at the end of each chapter. It offers hope that its readers will be inspired to take a closer look at what is considered normal in our families, communities and cities and identify dysfunctional influences or behaviors that numb our responses and cloud our perceptions of what is normal sexual behavior versus abuse.

You should read this book to help you discover what you can do, given your own limitations and expectations, to prevent sexual abuse.

What Does This Book Discuss?

The main message of *Shielding Our Innocents* hinges on preventing child sexual abuse through education and by developing a personalized prevention plan. This book discusses the impact of sexual abuse coupled with other societal dysfunctions -- emphasizing its potential to continue to devastate. It also defines the behaviors sexual abuse encompasses. *Shielding Our Innocents* discusses all these things plus gives adult readers true interviews, within which some readers may be able to identify or discover additional solutions. Prevention checklists -- suggestions on prevention strategies, can be found at the end of each chapter.

The stories of the survivors and offenders detailed in *Shielding Our Innocents* are tremendously sad like all accounts of sexual abuse; however, their use in this book offers us empowerment over current and future offenders -- direction over our own fears. The interviews offer us sanction to protect our children because they inspire solutions and a wake-up call for the misinformed or uninformed. I could have written a book on preventing child sexual assault with no interviews, but these interviews are included because they illustrate the manipulations and denials offenders commonly use on children and demonstrate different ways survivors cope. Some cope and heal, while others cope by festering as their supposed protectors flounder with replies that include denial or frenzy or compassion with no solutions or solutions that work only under certain circumstances or only after someone has offended or has been offended. By understanding the beginnings of how offenders evolve and which opportunities he or she uses to offend, we can come up with a plan to prevent.

We can stop the evolutions of offenders by learning to deal with life experiences -- in poverty or wealth in more functionally healthy ways and by taking responsible actions around children to eliminate violent influences from our homes and neighborhoods. This book also discusses the impact of sexually explicit material found in some advertising, in the media, movies and some cartoons. These things may cloud our perceptions of what healthy sexual behavior is.

Who Are The Experts?

The experts in this book are the survivors, doctors and therapists of victims and offenders. Experts of sexual abuse are even the offenders themselves. Their voices are united here.

In *Shielding Our Innocents*, North Carolina psychologist Dr. William Tyson discusses sexual offenders and related problems of sexual abuse. Other experts in this field volunteered their comments to assist me in the objectives of this book. Psychologists Dr. Mark Douglas Everson and Dr. Barbara Walling Boat share their thoughts as well. Counselor Robert Hayes and other interviewees provide extensive details about the effects of sexual abuse and offer ways to prevent it.

The answers on how to go about preventing crimes of this nature are derived from what we are able to learn from the survivors and offenders themselves. A survivor often develops something of a sixth sense about others who have been victimized. Their concerns about the safety of others can be overwhelming for them and misunderstood by others.

Where Do We Start To Make A Difference?

Childhood. Childhood is the shortest period in our lives, and it is the time that influences the rest of our lives. Childhoods follow us in memories, in lessons loved and hated. For the survivor of child sexual abuse, memories are nightmares carried behind eyes and mouths that learn to hide truths in order to survive. We can start our quest to prevent sexual abuse by seeking understanding of normal child development. We can also help by learning what childrens' emotional needs are by getting to know them. Open doors of communication and reading updated information on childhood are steps toward prevention. This book only makes this suggestion and does not explore child development in detail.

You don't have to become a psychiatrist or psychologist to understand your child or children, but these professionals certainly can and do help us if we actually seek out information and use it. Books on childhood development by Louise Bates Ames, Ph.D and Frances L. Ilg, M.D. (*YOUR TWO-YEAR-OLD, YOUR THREE-YEAR-OLD, YOUR FOUR-YEAR-OLD* and more) or *Dr. Spock's Baby and Child Care* by Benjamin Spock, M.D. and Michael B. Rothenberg, M.D. are good places to start for this.

The creativity that is inspired during childhood to build castles of adventure and fun is destroyed by waves of intrusion and violation by offenders, and this is what survivors remember. For survivors, creativity is used for designing ways to survive emotionally in environments that do not render themselves trustworthy and functionally healthy enough to tell. For survivors, creativity is also used in designing ways to survive within the habitats of their own minds. By understanding our children -- being their best friends, and knowing what is normal for whatever stage they are at, we will be more sensitive if something as disruptive to a child's development as sexual abuse is, attempts to intrude.

In order to design a plan of prevention, it is imperative that we understand the current dilemma victims and survivors are facing. We can create safe emotional havens for them -- devoid of criticism, harsh and unfair judgment. It is only a fraction of the solution. I hope this book will provide victims with some of the emotional benefits and nurturing they may be seeking, and I hope other readers will be inspired to take action to prevent.

How Can We Prevent
The Sexual Assault Of Our Innocents?

We can stop sexual abuse offenders by using what we know about dysfunctional patterns in regard to violence in general and sexual offenders. We can also, as emphasized by the National Committee to Prevent Child Abuse, prevent child abuse in all forms by reaching out and helping parents under stress or suspected stress and by getting help for yourself if you have difficulty raising your child or children. *

Chapter III: Sexual Offenders -- Who Are They? provides details, some of which, you may know and some you may have never heard of before, to give you specific opportunities offenders rely on in order to offend. It also verbally demonstrates -- paints pictures, through the interviews the cyclical damages of abuse. The interviews show how abuse and violence disrupts the emotional healthy development of children. (See *Chapter II: Individual Recollections From Adult Survivors.*) By stopping physical abuse, emotional abuse and other domestic violence, the likelihood of stopping alcoholism, drug abuse and sexual abuse is strengthened. If you plug up a tunnel a mouse has made into your home, you decrease the likelihood of more mice or the same mouse returning. By solving problems that often overlap sexual abuse, we can stop sexual abuse from ever occurring.

The interviews with the victims are open and honest. The survivors I spoke face-to-face with often needed assurance that I understood their fears of being labeled or misunderstood no matter how shocking their stories were. The child molesters I interviewed were primarily comprised of regressed sexual offenders and pedophiles. Their stories are not provided for the sake of sensationalism or hype, as I talk about later in this book. They bring us down to earth, so to speak, for a closer examination of truth. They bolster more than our compassion; hopefully more solutions than the ones suggested in this book.

Victims of sexual abuse are often treated inappropriately by family members, juries and court officials. Increased public awareness through education and the media is progress, but there are still many who would benefit by reading not only this book, but by actually attending the court trials involving sexual abuse cases or by befriending a victim they may know.

This book also provides a list of references and notes, and these sources offer answers and hope for healing as well.

Caring adults can use suggestions and ideas in this book to protect their children and to teach them how to protect themselves. They can also benefit from the book by learning warning signs of potential abuse. Obviously, this book is not appropriate reading for children.

Catch-22 Situations Stifle Progress

"The maltreatment of children robs our communities of healthy, thriving girls and boys -- youngsters who may never become responsible, productive adults.

"And for every child who is injured, humiliated, or killed as the result of abuse, the human costs -- the physical and emotional anguish -- are incalculable."
{ Source: A pamphlet: *"It shouldn't hurt to be a child,"* by the North Carolina Chapter of the National Committee to Prevent Child Abuse.* Reprinted with permission. }

Sometimes the position and power of an individual to make a difference is stifled by another's misuse of position, power and influence. You have probably experienced this when your good intentions to help someone in need were thwarted by another's whose beliefs were based on false information or just differed from yours.

During the 1980s, I observed court and wrote articles on Superior Court cases in North Carolina. I covered cases involving defendants who were accused of molesting and/or raping children between the ages of 5 and 13. While reporting, I often saw a lack of communication between victims and officials who were supposed to be helping child victims. Some of these adults portrayed themselves as (and believed themselves to be) friends of sexually abused children. On the sidelines, they occasionally expressed what I later came to view as dysfunctional beliefs and attitudes. The hypocrisy was somehow camouflaged by career titles -- positions of authority and personal recognition goals.

An attorney, for example, expressed to me a belief that victims of sexual molestation were better off living with the offender when the offender happened to be their primary breadwinner. This particular attorney expressed that such beliefs were reasonable even if the *breadwinner/offender* was the mother's live-in boyfriend. He did not stand alone. A female editor expressed to me disbelief also about young children who claimed to have been molested.

{A bit of irony here is that women are commonly seen as protectors of children, and in previous decades, as the primary caretakers of children. In many societies, including those in the United States, women are the last to be suspected among their peers of abusing a child sexually. Women are, in general, the ones to bathe, feed, play with and comfort children. Women are socialized in some families to take on such responsibilities as adults.}

I still have a problem with the editor who told me to stick to the skeleton of sexual abuse cases (e.g. defendant's name, age, address, charge, plea, judgment, sentence) and to stop offending the paper's readers with too many details about sexual abuse cases -- the childrens' court testimony, actual quotes. She told me to leave such details for murder, robbery cases and the like. I butted heads with her several times on many issues, so I went about my business still stumbling onto more sexual abuse cases and reporting the details anyway.

Understanding what is involved in crimes against children is emotionally difficult for most of us -- especially when others are always trying to set limits on just how much we can do to help by throwing their own denial-fear tactics into our pathways.

The hairs on my arms stood in thousands of goosebumps -- company to nausea, as I sat in courtrooms gazing at the profiles of offenders and their sometimes tactless mannerisms. In my private thoughts, I saw the editor (and others like her who tried to convince me openly that the victims were probably lying) as a sort of "offender." She offended me by trying to shut me up! After all, journalism is about reporting truths; even painful ones.

I realized the editor who attempted to silence me represented a sample of dysfunctional attitudes -- removed from the goals of reporting truth. Her fears and outside influences in a small town had infected her abilities to see the truth like TB affecting one's ability to breathe adequately because of a refusal to take a full course of antibiotics.

Offenders hide in the fears of their victims, and they hide in the shadows of our own fears and expectations. We cannot effectively cope without lancing the infected wounds of past generations. Dysfunction within families breeds dysfunction throughout society. Sometimes, even dysfunctional thinking -- thinking that prevents a person from truthfully sympathizing or reasoning that attempts to cover sexual abuse wounds with a sheet and pretend they are not there, ministers to the least suspecting occupations. Nothing gets resolved, and problems are passed on.

Victims need not only the assistance of protective agencies and their legal guardians, they need to have the newspapers that cover their stories speak truths and provide an adequate voice for them. Reporters and writers need to practice great sensitivity when dealing with these kinds of news stories. They should report facts with the understanding that exposing the offender's actions, and the effects such actions can lead to, is in itself, a sort of therapy for society too.

It is not a matter of exposing the victim. That is sensationalism. The victim in every case, I believe, should be protected by the press, legal officials, friends and family members from any public criticisms, scurrilities or misunderstandings. Their names should never be used, but their voices -- their quotes should be conveyed accurately. Truthful portrayals of sexual abuse cases are part of the education we receive about sexual abuse. Conscientious and scrupulous education is part of the motivation we should use to stop offenders.

Yellow journalism is not part of the education I am speaking of. Yellow journalism is not only telling an untruth through the published word, but it is the conscious effort to conceal the truth. Yellow journalism tactics where sexual abuse cases are concerned perpetuate social ignorance and further entrap its readers with opinions based on false information. This takes root in other things as well: our families, schools and churches.

Catch-22 situations or conundrums can take on the form of scapegoating as part of the victim's overall experience if or when he or she decides to tell someone or report the offender. Even if the offender is never reported to authorities outside of his or her family, scapegoating still takes place and furthermore compounds the catch-22 situation. It becomes one of the things that hinders new resolutions and barricades old ones.

Victims of sexual abuse are not only scapegoated by some public officials, but by family members as well. For instance, in cases of incest, some family members may turn against the offended when the abuse is unveiled. They may act hostile with the victim or directly or indirectly blame and/or ignore the complaints.

Some feel they must take sides in cases of incest. They are afraid of admitting belief because to do so, they believe they are saying their family is not important and that they must stop loving the offender if they choose to believe the victim's claims. Family members may attempt to discredit the victim's claims by supporting disbelief with notions that the victim has lied about other things or the victim is too emotional or illogical to believe.

Despite laws society imposes, some people in the United States and in cultures around the world, in addition, may subconsciously or consciously view sexual contact between a female child and an adult man as harmless. On the other hand, these same people may see sexual contact between an adult and a male child as unnatural and therefore, a criminal act. These attitudes fester and incubate potentially overwhelming problems for victims. Attitudes about child sexual abuse play an active role in how victims deal with bad experiences. Experiences, good and bad, and attitudes and conclusions that evolve from them, contribute to shaping our personalities.

Derek Jehu in his book, *Beyond Sexual Abuse, Therapy With Women Who Were Childhood Victims* describes the effects dysfunctional attitudes can have on the victim and on those the victims confide in:

"... she is 'rocking the boat' of an allegedly close family system, threatening its survival, and perhaps evoking guilt in its members for not protecting the victim ... In adulthood, many incest victims report reactions of anger ... Grief reactions have also been reported among previously sexually abused women." * { Source: *Beyond Sexual Abuse, Therapy With Women Who Were Childhood Victims* by Derek Jehu. Copyright (c) 1988 by John Wiley & Sons, Ltd. Reproduced with permission of the publisher. }

Jehu points out that adult women who experienced sexual abuse as children are faced with a sense of loss and a psychological death. Survivors of child sexual abuse go through a grieving process, which is essential to coping and healing. It is easy to conclude that the problems of child molestation often linger into adulthood. There are people who choose to believe an adult over a child or simply ignore the real problems of molestation, regardless of what they really believe or know as fact and sometimes regardless of whether the victimization is disclosed by an adult who experienced it as a child.

Many times those who learn of the molestations do not understand why some victims -- no matter what their ages may be, did not attempt to tell an adult after being molested initially or why they did not stand up and fight back. Non-victims sometimes do not know how easy it is for adult perpetrators in positions of authority to manipulate a child and how cumbersome it is for a child who is told, "*Good children always obey adults. Good children are not to question authority. Good children do what they are told. Bad children get everyone upset.*" In addition, children often do not even understand the actions of their offenders. These messages may make the child feel responsible for the molestation.

By empowering our children with information about sexual abuse -- information appropriate for their ages, and instilling a sense of importance and self-worth through mutual respect, care and love, we give them added protection against sexual abuse. By empowering ourselves with information, we can better control the sorts of influences that may rob our children of their own sense of self-worth.

We can block potential influences that can dictate to children a sense of being less valuable. Peer pressure to conform to some of society's oddities represented by the media, in sexually explicit advertising, violent cartoons and movies influence children, so it is reasonable that parents should use healthy influences of stable home, church and school environments to redirect their children. Violence and explicit sexual scenes on television should not be part of the curriculum for raising children, but it is found easily on day-time television and within our families in the ways we choose to deal with stress or daily problems. These things add weight to sinking ships, and it is our own consciousness and utilization of information that is going to prevent dysfunctional patterns from continuing.

CHAPTER

"And whoever welcomes a little child like this in my name welcomes me. But if anyone causes one of these little ones who believe in me to sin, it would be better for him to have a large millstone hung around his neck and to be drowned in the depths of the sea." -- Matthew 18:05-06. *(NIV)*.

A Discussion On Prevention, Help And Forgiveness

Prevention is calculated, planned and direct action that unblocks doorways and portals, delivering illumination onto the obstacle -- risks of it occurring and outcomes for those who have survived. Prevention of sexual abuse is about preventing domestic violence, alcoholism, drug abuse, physical and emotional child and spousal abuse. These things are often the tangled knots that forecast the likelihood of sexual abuse occurring.

Sexual abuse is an uncomfortable and embarrassing topic for most everyone to think about and discuss, but it is a horrifically uncomfortable situation for thousands of survivors and victims yet to be discovered, saved from further harm and comforted, if ever. It continues in face of everything that we know about victims and offenders. It continues because information about prevention, such as eliminating opportunities for offenders, is not being thoroughly and consistently circulated and then implemented into what we teach children at home and in schools. It thrives as child protectors carry on in face of being undermined by the general acceptance of other sorts of violence, which are easily seen by surfing through the television channels. Efforts are undermined too when domestic violence -- yelling, screaming, hitting and worse, continues down a parallel track.

Child sexual abuse includes many sorts of preventable actions: the fondling of private body parts or touching with a sexual intent, indecent exposure or exhibitionism, exposing children to pornographic materials, deliberately exposing a child to the act of sexual intercourse, masturbation in front of a child, forcing or coercing a child to touch an adult's sexual organs, any penetration of a child's vagina or anus no matter how slight by a penis or other body parts, such as fingers or by the use of objects. Sexual abuse is often a progressing pattern that puts children in situations that can lead to pregnancy, disease, suicide, eating disorders, emotional problems, mistrust of others, poor grades or extreme changes in school grade performance, etc. (See *Chapter IV: What Are The Signs Of Sexual Abuse?*)

Tuning In/Tuning Out Media Influences

If we understand which high risk behaviors strengthen the likelihood of sexual abuse, then we should also look at the things that influence our attitudes about violence. How can we rid our society of its sexual offenders if we are fed attitudes of acceptance in regard to television violence? How can we be effective in our efforts while falling under the influences of sexually explicit movies and advertisements using sex to sell products? I am not saying that television violence and advertisements with provocative and intentional sexual overtones directly cause child sexual assault; however, I am saying that these influences are counterproductive in terms of getting anyone to make any meaningful changes concerning the messages that are tolerated and consumed today by readers and audiences -- people who can take steps to prevent sexual abuse.

Advertisements with sexual overtones are available to children on a daily basis on television and in magazines. Why should advertising or movie or story plots filled with violence and sex have to be part of our culture? We should question what we have come to accept as normal. There is a place for documentaries and movie histories of past and present social, political and familial expressions within our cultural needs and framework; however, my question is why do we give so much attention to entertaining ourselves with fictional violence and cruelties?

Violence in fictional movies and in other mediums provides unhealthy influences particularly for offenders or potential offenders. These things cloud society's ideas and conclusions about what is considered deviant versus normal or moral behavior. Some television violence promotes unhealthy role models whose acting skills are used to glorify the act of hurting another human being. As individuals and a society, we have to be careful about what we approve of as acceptable.

We intellectually understand that sexual abuse is evil; however, we may react phlegmatically or untouched when we read about sexual abuse cases on a daily basis. The cases seem removed from readers because most readers do not know the people they read about, and there always seems to be a new case. Indifference and unsympathetic emotional regards take less energy. Then, there are those who enjoy gossip -- the news sexual abuse cases inspire. Gossiping expends a lot of energy. These attitudes hinder our human experiences to promote and insure emotionally and physically safe environments for children.

The media has a responsibility to our young and old to provide up-to-date information about many issues. Readers, viewers and listeners have a responsibility to voice opinions, written or otherwise, about what we are not going to accept. Nonresistant and complaisant attitudes about television violence and advertising with sexually explicit scenes sets us up to fail. We fail -- personally, if or when we discover our children have been sexually abused, or impersonally, when we pick up the newspaper and read about another statistic. The media speaks all sorts of truths about the violence that occurs behind closed doors, on our streets, in our faces and in schools, our parks, our churches. These reports are important.

The media speaks many truths about the sorts of sexual appetites we believe as being normal in the advertisements we read. They dictate, however, what we want to believe too. We hear about violence in the news, and then we entertain ourselves by watching fictional shows that reinforce the idea that violence is a normal part of living.

Sex and violence are the focal points -- the hub of society's entertainment desires. I believe these things have been fed to us through entertainment in small quantities until the quantities have accumulated into ridiculous portions many of us would not have accepted in the movies fifty or sixty years ago. Although violence can easily be found in truth such as Biblical histories and in Shakespearean plays and literature, the impact of television violence for the sake of entertainment is far greater -- especially on children who are not mature enough to make distinctions between fictional and non-fictional television broadcasts.

Violence during wartimes in terms of defending ourselves has surely been a large part of our culture, and these things have an influence on us. We are the most intelligent of life forms. We have the ability to find and use non-violent forms of defense at home and afar. We also have the ability to find and use forms of entertainment that do not include sexual exploitation. It starts with what we define as acceptable and by what we will continue to tolerate in the entertainment and advertising fields. Becoming more attuned to what we allow to influence our decisions and 'to see the cake without the frosting' will have a direct impact on our ability to control sexually deviant people and prevent sexual abuse.

If you want to nurture a child into adolescence and adulthood, you provide food, shelter and appropriate clothing, vaccinations, safety apparatuses, good schools and experiences. We want good results. Part of this love and guidance is guarding children and ourselves from unhealthy influences so that if or when we have to discern a situation we might otherwise be unsure of, we will be able to find the right answers quickly and not be fooled by would-be offenders. This sort of control can only go so far.

It's difficult to protect our children and ourselves from media magnetisms we experience just walking to a bus stop or shopping or reading. We need the media. It needs us. But, we need to exercise our voices more through the media about what we find as unacceptable in children's movies, cartoons and in regular magazine and television ads. Our society can appear unconcerned at times. It flounders around -- attempting to do something, but its voices fade, and the listeners turn up the rap so no one can hear! Is this living?

Living has to do with life, and violence is about death -- emotionally, intellectually and physically. Living should be about surviving through loving works and deeds, enjoyment; not surviving by learning tactics to avoid another's evil deeds. This is what the sexually abused learn. But, this is what it has boiled down to: *What can we do to avoid falling prey to another's deviant behaviors? What can we do to keep the molester away from our children -- away from us and out of our lives?* Does this sound like a desperate plea? We are a desperate society with bolted doors -- inside a catch-22 situation. Some of us prefer the blindfolds, earplugs to comfort our fears instead of facing truth and changing it to a truth we can live with and not continuing on with one we can pretend with.

Victims of sexual abuse are often desperate, but rarely plead directly to those who could prevent such crimes. They sometimes plead with themselves to find a way to forget until they finally find a way to cope and heal or cope and fester. Some survivors plead with their offenders to stop long after the offender's ears have died with the rest of him or her.

Survivors hide from you and themselves. The actions of their offenders live in their emotional deaths. Survivors live a life of pretending that they were not offended or that the offenses did not occur. Escaping this dilemma takes fortitude and discipline, and prevention requires the same formula. Prevention is the best answer to at least decreasing the number of reported and unreported cases of sexual abuse. Putting an end to television violence and some of the sexual messages some industries use to sell products would help -- but will this happen?

So much of the world is caught up in what it believes it is, and does not see the hypocrisy it indulges in. Well, maybe it does, and could care less! On the one hand, one tobacco company shouts it is concerned about underage smoking, while it continues to advertise cigarettes to adults who smoke them in front of children. These children then may grow up with the condoning attitude that smoking is okay as long as you are an adult. The same hypocritical attitudes are pushed in movies too. Adult movies depicting sexual violence are seen as okay as long as the viewing audience is restricted to adults. Children who are sexually victimized by adults may be guarded from the immediate influences of Rated R movies, but in the long run, are they guarded from the adults who are influenced by such movies?

Getting the right information about what sexual abuse is and how it affects children and adults in the short and long runs is a first step to preventing child sexual assault. Ridding our minds of the clutter influences of the sexual violence incorporated into fictional movies and some music might do us some good too.

Protecting Your Real Assets, Our Children

Education on preventing sexual abuse unlocks the door that so often isolates us from truths surrounding sexual assault. Implementing prevention into our lives, making it part of the education we need to survive and part of the education we give our children is another step to preventing sexual abuse. This turns the knob of the door labeled: "Get Wise. Protect Your Real Assets, Our Children."

Of course, reporting suspicions of child sexual abuse to the police and/or to social services and other authorities is another step of prevention, and this, in itself, can prevent further incidents of abuse and may stop perpetrators from abusing others.

We cannot stagnate our abilities to rescue children. We must not trap ourselves with fears and anxieties about reporting suspicions of sexual abuse. We cannot continue under the comforting notion that someone else will take care of those wounded by sexual abuse. We can influence a better outcome for survivors and victims and for our children. Families can start using the information available consistently and conscientiously to prevent violence of all forms.

Different forms of violence (e.g. on television cartoons, fictional murder and robbery shows, domestic and social violence) reinforce dysfunctional thinking -- thinking that provides easy roads to sexual abuse in dysfunctional families, where alcoholism, drug abuse, prior unresolved emotional traumas or childhood abuse is present. The core of sexual abuse is dysfunctional, unhealthy thinking that evolves into dysfunctional behaviors, and the dysfunctional mind has been influenced by dysfunctional behavior many times before -- most likely during childhood.

Anyone with the knowledge of, or suspicion of, a child being abused who ignores or even expects someone else to bandage this problem, is wrong and part of the problem. It is imperative that the damages of past generations not dictate to current and future families a cycle of abuse that emotionally maimed societies before us. Getting a better understanding of ourselves and how all sorts of violence affects us will help us understand how to use the knowledge we obtain on prevention.

Decreasing Odds Of Abuse By Strengthening Self-Esteem

Self-esteem can influence the outcome of many situations. How people see themselves can make the difference between success and failure. Do you view yourself as weak or strong, intelligent or threatened, a victim or a survivor? Whatever adjectives people use to describe themselves may be different, depending upon who they are relaying the information to, but when we are alone, are we able to be honest with ourselves?

Victims of sexual assault are denied a normal sense of self-worth because the crime dictates messages of being worthless -- not worthy of being treated as a valuable person. Even though some survivors may seek up-the-ladder careers and advanced education, these goals are often thwarted because of how survivors come to view themselves. They become trapped by these feelings if there are no other comforting and safe avenues to rescue them. They develop their own defenses or projected images to distract others from suspecting they have been used, robbed of their childhoods and feelings of self-worth and esteem. And if they appear to be at peace with the world and themselves, their real world is isolated and lonely.

Building high self-esteem in your child -- praising his successes and his attempts, gives children added protection against sexual abuse. Commending him for trying, even when he fails, is a step to building a good self-image, and this is so important for strengthening good character. When self-esteem is low, people are vulnerable and easily manipulated by others looking to prey on them. Encouraging a sense of importance and self-value instills personal trust. Give your child the building blocks and the coat of armor he needs by telling him routinely that he is loved.

Show him he is loved by listening to his ideas, praising his efforts at school and with home tasks. Listen to him when he talks to you. Treat him with the same respect you would a fellow adult or as you would like to be regarded. Include him in your conversations and never give him any reason to think you would not protect him.

Do not hit your children or punish them by whipping them with belts, switches, canes, hairbrushes, crops or rulers. Guard his emotional health as much as you would his physical well-being. Constant belittling and criticisms or name calling has become so immersed into the lives of some that people have become insensitive to how it actually affects a child's feelings of worth, and feelings of worth come from feeling safe -- physically and psychologically.

The environment children are raised in often times dictates feelings of worth or worthlessness -- depending on how children are taught to regard themselves. Hitting a child guarantees notions that if you are bigger than another, then it is okay to hit.

There may be circumstances that threaten potentially deadly situations, and these situations may warrant *no more than one* smack on the legs or hand to get a child's attention, but even this method must be done with extreme care in informing the child of your intentions of warning them of danger -- not to run into the street or traffic, not to play with matches or fire, not to play with toys near a stove, to keep seat belts on while the car is in operation, etc. and such punishment should never leave bruises, cuts, welts or physical and emotional injuries, which can leave children more vulnerable to sexual abuse. Physical punishment always lends itself to the possibility of the administrator getting out of control. I believe; however, that alternative non-violent methods of discipline are to everyone's advantage.

The best method of teaching children is through example -- modeling the correct behavior. I have read this advice dozens of times in parents' magazines and brochures on children. I implemented them into my life, and it is difficult given the sorts of dysfunctions that seem to dominate our society -- in media violence and language and in our own childhood memories. It would be hypocritical for me to even hint at being a perfect parent. I do the wrong thing sometimes -- within the legal parameters, but start over, struggling to rid my own socialization of dysfunctional anger. It is difficult to fight and prevent dysfunction that attaches to every member of society like feathers to glue, but creating an emotionally safe home environment is a first step to preventing child sexual assault.

As adults, we must seek to understand that using violent forms of punishment "*to teach*" or "*to control*" our children is wrong. Sex offenders have reported that they were beaten as children or viewed violent forms of punishment while growing up. If we accept violence as a reasonable means of control, we are inviting more of the same. Somewhere down the line it returns. Its return is often toxic.

Preventing Opportunity

Allowing dysfunctional behaviors to continue fuels new dysfunctions and results in more victims. To stop abuse, we must make a conscious effort to do so. Prevention is never passive. Children who feel safe and accepted with and by their parents are more likely to reveal even the threat of sexual assault. They are more likely not to appear as vulnerable to the emotional manipulation of opportunistic offenders, who look for signs of lonely or isolated children. Opportunistic offenders, particularly pedophiles, look for roles they can play in order to actualize their fantasies. (Read more about this in *Chapter III: Sexual Offenders -- Who Are They?*)

While researching and writing this book, I have learned that adult survivors of sexual abuse were sometimes beaten, criticized or ignored by people -- their parents or other caretakers, whose actions walled off potential functional communication for the victims. The threat of criticism or of being beaten by people unrelated and uninformed of the sexual abuse, isolated the victims even more, giving the offender more opportunity and power to continue. Offenders target children they can easily manipulate into secrecy. They use children's worst fears to frighten them into silence: *"Your parents will hate you."* or *"Your parents would never believe you."* or they simply misuse an adult position of authority and warn their victims: *"Don't tell anybody!"* They capitalize on the fears children already have about the possibility of upsetting people or being hated or disliked.

We should not, as parents and caretakers, blindly put our children in catch-22 situations. Although we learn many things in life about morals and what is right, good, etc., understanding this intellectually and actually implementing these things is a deepseated process that begins in childhood. What we know intellectually does not always match what we do. Our childhood experiences can dictate to us otherwise. If parents tell their children they love them, and then beat them, then the likelihood of that child ever discovering what love really is is clouded.

Conflicting Social Lessons Hinder Prevention

Survivors of sexual abuse often make poor choices in their adult lives based on the information and experiences they are given as children. They make decisions based on fear and familiarity instead of being based on what they really want or on logic. Women survivors of childhood sexual assault sometimes end up in relationships with men who abuse them in other ways. It is difficult for anyone to make the right decisions in life if their upbringing is a hodgepodge of conflicting intellectual lessons: *"Honor your father and mother...,"* (Ephesians 6:02, [NIV]) or *"Fathers, do not exasperate your children; instead, bring them up in the training and instruction of the Lord."* (Ephesians 6:04, [NIV]) and then experiencing parents who scream and curse at their offspring or who beat, belittle, lie to or humiliate.

"Thou shalt not commit adultery" and *"Thou shalt not murder"* are other important intellectual lessons that are undermined if or when a caretaker or parent condones or allows their children, for example, to view films that reinforce the idea that sex outside of marriage is okay as long as it is safe sex or that watching someone murder someone on television is okay because television violence is only fictional or pretend.

An actor, to my noted attention, said once that he was guilty of a lot of things, but never adultery. The actor, a prominent womanizer, surely did not understand the true meaning of adultery. It applies to even our thoughts. Teaching children what is acceptable begins with modeling the proper behavior, setting *"intellectual"* guidelines, informing them of penalties for breaking rules and laws. Doing all these things in a loving, reassuring environment will give added protection from sexual abuse because these things do not threaten, maim or destroy self-esteem.

Parents and caretakers need to build strong relationships with children -- relationships devoid of double messages, so that children will not continue being easy prey for opportunistic offenders. I say opportunistic offenders because offenders look for opportunities to abuse children with their pestilent fantasies, and such opportunities may be as simple as a visit to a relative's or neighbor's or friend's house, to public or private restrooms or to the park or store. For some offenders, opportunities present themselves within their own families.

Some offenders rely on their position within families to get away with offending our innocents. Of course, the likelihood of sexual abuse, as well as other sorts of abuse, are increased when children are left alone with or in the care of an alcoholic or drug abuser; however, offenders can be anybody. They can be doctors, lawyers, businessmen, chemists, farmers, mill workers, neighbors, relatives, and the use or abuse of alcohol and/or drugs are not always what precipitates the assaults. Offenders zero in on children who appear vulnerable -- children with inattentive parents or caretakers or isolated children who demonstrate very compliant or non-resistant behavior towards adults or other children -- children whose physical language suggests that they would be easily intimidated or quiet or overwhelmed with the notion that adults should always be obeyed.

Children need experiences in life that build healthy self-esteem and that foster loving, trustworthy and responsible behaving relationships -- relationships children can emotionally and intellectually depend on if ever confronted with a would-be offender or if ever actually assaulted. Children need environments that foster a feeling of open communication, so that in the event of sexual assault or threat of assault, children will feel free to run to the authorities and/or a protective confidant and fight back or to shout, "*No! Leave me alone!*" and not feel trapped by rules for obeying elders. Some children are left helpless because they have been taught they should *always, no matter what,* respect others who are older. Building self-confidence and good self-esteem is to make home life into a place, where a child always feels accepted, a place he can play and learn, sleep and eat without the dysfunctions of the world outside of our homes influencing behavior to our disadvantage. Children need home environments that are devoid of arrogance. They need homes that foster feelings of security: love, trust, happiness, and constructive guidance -- not homes filled with emotional war games that wreak havoc on the familial socialization experiences of children. Offenders take advantage of situations they can hide behind. If the victim is usually scapegoated by family members for things unrelated to sexual abuse, and the offender observes this or even senses this, the offender uses this knowledge for his or her goals.

Offenders sometimes use tactics that trick children into believing they are their friends by giving them gifts or by doing favors for them. Offenders may do this prior to the actual abuse or afterwards or as a sort of bribe or coercion. This sort of trickery leaves children feeling that they are responsible for abuse they experience. It might be easier for a child to believe the claims of an offender if the child's home life experiences undermine a child's feelings of trust and importance.

An offender might attempt to convince a child that he is his or her only friend or the offender's social or familial relationship to the child may imply trust. Offenders are craftsmen at taking advantage of a child's trust (and of those who really love and care for the child) and then instilling fears that telling would cause more problems for the child. Children's caretakers and parents should provide ongoing information and education on self-protection and age-appropriate information on safety and demonstrated or hidden dangers in our society. Sharing this sort of information gives children a feeling of being in control and raises self-esteem.

The manner in which children are treated and the amount of respect for another that is demonstrated speak louder lessons than words of guidance. Words of violence, on the other hand, wound a child's spirit and heart. All these things influence us as children and as adults. Home is not an emotionally safe place for some children. It is not a place, where the abused can feel completely honest with the way they feel about anything without the potential danger of being sharply criticized or misunderstood. The overall atmospheres that some parents or caretakers create at home do not lend themselves to the sort of consistency of atmosphere children would feel safe in telling their parents or caretakers about having been sexually abused, or even about the threat of sexual abuse.

Criticism still hurts adults, as many of us know. It has taken some of us all of our lives to realize that we are entitled and allowed to speak our minds, express our fears and call for help if or when we need it. We are deserving of love and respect. Children may know these things intellectually, but they may not believe them if their home or caretaking environments render instability of physical and emotional respect.

Children are easy to love, so it is not understandable that so many are misunderstood and abused at home and at school and then discounted and not believed when stories of sexual abuse get even a glimpse at voicing themselves. Children are taught just how much they are loved by their families first, then at school. Some of the survivors and offenders I interviewed for this book expressed that neither of these places were happy places while growing up. They experienced a universal truth: Attitudes of love are reflected from parents to child, and the feelings this creates in a child are perceived by peers, and this perception of oneself is eventually mirrored back to the child from peers. The biblical lesson: "*Love your neighbor as yourself*" often takes a back seat to this. If parents are unable to communicate love to a child in a manner that makes the child feel truly safe and provide that child with experiences that bring heartfelt security words can hardly describe, then that child's risk for low self-esteem is increased. What is mirrored back and forth to and from the child, parents and peers then reinforces feelings of worthlessness and self-hatred, or the feeling that "*There must be something wrong with me from the very beginning*" in the child.

Victims of any sort of child abuse, particularly sexual abuse, learn to accommodate their feelings and thoughts by hiding them. They learn to accommodate the behavior of the people around them in order to avoid confrontation or criticism. They find criticism from parents or others painful and difficult to cope with, but they refrain from voicing this themselves. I think this is true of children of all generations who are part of a dysfunctional cycle. Children sometimes avoid revealing feelings and truths they feel will get them punished or criticized.

We can seek the understanding of children's fears by asking them quite openly and sincerely to share their feelings about their fears in general. By allowing them to verbalize fears, parents will obtain insights about their child that will help parents map out and use personalized prevention techniques. If a child expresses a dislike or persistent fear or complaint of dislike for certain caretakers by misbehaving, try to find out beyond surface appearances if there is something else troubling the child. The problem could be the caretaker.

Helping Survivors

There are layers of social problems we must peel off to get to the seeds of sexual abuse. To find compassion for the drug abuser, alcoholic, spousal and child abuser is in itself a mountain, but success in the healing of these things would prevent sexual abuse in many cases from ever occurring. Helping survivors through their isolation and fears will contribute much in terms of stopping dysfunctional patterns. If the crime of sexual abuse occurs despite efforts of prevention or if it occurs or occurred many years ago, survivors should first acknowledge that they at least survived. They should also acknowledge that the abuse they endured was no fault of their own in any way. Survivors need to understand that they should be very selective in choosing confidantes who are sensitive to their emotional needs and hurts.

A survivor who tells just anyone out of an urgent need to rid themselves of the stress of holding everything in or of prolonged emotional accommodation of an offender's impositions will risk sharp criticism and rejection. Some of the survivors I interviewed while writing this book (See *Chapter II: Individual Recollections From Adult Survivors*) told of horrible accounts of double betrayal experiences -- first as children being victimized by a person they were socialized to trust, and then years later, by insensitive ears that happened into the auditory pathway of a survivor struggling to cope alone by reaching out to someone. What an injustice and a sad fact this is! Survivors need and should be believed. It is through survivors we are able to learn what it is we are really up against.

Healing is a day-by-day task, and victims should never expect to ever feel the same as prior to being abused. What they can eventually feel is happiness in forgiveness, and happiness that by sharing their stories with other survivors, they are helping others not feel isolated any longer. They will help themselves and others to understand that simply talking about the past with a trusting and caring individual or another survivor will bring about understanding of oneself and reasons for choices made during and since the abuse.

Talking about the experiences or writing about them will help survivors find the anger they themselves suppressed and camouflaged with guilt and self-hate, which may have also been camouflaged with outward mannerisms and words that suggested: "*All is right with me and the world.*" These things will help survivors identify their offenders even if not by name, but position or relationship to them. It will help survivors identify their offenders to themselves as the offenders actually are -- not just as depressed, sick individuals, but as the person or people who managed to fool responsible adults while hiding their deeds in the safety of a child's fears. Some victims feel guilty for hating those who offended them. They feel ambivalence because they are taught that feelings of disliking a relative or friend of the family is wrong, and then such victims feel trapped and immobile -- unable to disclose sexual assault or even the threat of it. The offender causes countless hurts for victims and survivors.

There are many ideas on how to go about healing oneself. I have included quotes from interviews I have done with professionals specializing in counseling survivors and others. If you are a survivor, I hope you will find some stepping stones here to resolving your own burdens. I have included, as you will find, varying opinions on dealing with sexual abuse memories. It is important to present the varying opinions, I feel, because what initially works for one survivor may not for another.

Where Should Survivors Seek Help? / What Does This Involve?

Survivors need a strong network of emotional support. This support might come from a spouse, parents, aunts, uncles, special friends, psychologists, doctors. Finding the right confidantes can be precipitated by prayer. My opinion is that prayer and faith in God are part of the first steps to cleansing hate and fear -- the kind that results from sexual abuse. This is a continuing process. An emotionally safe environment for disclosure is a mandatory part of a first step to healing. Talking with a trusted friend or professional is part of this too. Continued faith in God's healing and direction provides the sort of strength and spiritual support survivors need to journey through pasts and futures. Although some survivors may start with prayer, there are some who only begin to pray about their internal warfare associated with having been sexually abused after writing about it or reading about other survivor experiences. God works miracles through others -- counselors, trusted friends, ministers, psychologists and psychiatrists, among others. This book includes varying opinions in an attempt to show many avenues for healing. Whatever approach a survivor chooses, it should be compatible with his or her needs. Ages of children should be taken into consideration when seeking appropriate therapy or advice.

Some adult survivors of sexual abuse are not emotionally ready to commit themselves to therapy, and may find several years lapse until they feel up to it or ready to verbalize what happened during their childhoods. Survivors of sexual abuse can find direction in trustworthy confidantes, or by writing about their experiences and memories in a journal, in a diary or on paper they can destroy in private later. They eventually find comfort in forgiveness; not easily arrived at. How does all of this come about? Digging up the past and coming to terms with it is not an easy process. (Read *Chapter II: Individual Recollections From Adult Survivors* for more on how victims and survivors cope with and without outside help.)

Acceptance And Forgiveness

While researching and during the beginning stages of writing this book, I spoke with counselors and psychologists in an attempt to gain more understanding in the area of *"forgiveness"* and to make my research on sexual abuse more thorough. Therapist Robert Hayes of Charlotte, North Carolina was among those who volunteered to share facts, comments and opinions about forgiveness issues and other matters regarding sexual abuse histories.

As you read about the struggles survivors are saddled with, you will understand the deeper issues involved and how prevention of sexual abuse would eliminate needless suffering. I have included recovery steps he cited in this chapter. According to Hayes, recovery involves several steps -- steps that require the guidance of a sensitive and caring counselor.

Step One: Accept the total reality of your experience, including all emotional responses to it.

Step Two: Understand how your responses to the experience affected your development and current behavior.

Step Three: Identify changes you want to make.

Step Four: Set goals for accomplishing those changes.

In regard to forgiving the offender as an aspect of recovery, Hayes said: "*I think forgiveness is totally optional. It is not incumbent upon the victim to understand the need of the perpetrator. One of the things I tell the offenders in treatment when they start having contact with their victims is that under no circumstances are they to ask for forgiveness. If I slap you, and then I ask you to forgive me, then I am asking you to say what I did was all right.*

"*Up to a point, forgiveness is important,*" Hayes said. "*The victim needs to know that the person who victimized them has a problem -- but not so they can forgive the offender, but so they can forgive what happened. Forgiveness comes much later in recovery,"* Hayes said.

"The thing that comes first is dealing with the total reality of the experience, and anger is a big one. Anger is important. You can feel anger toward a person you love. You still feel anger over their actions..."

Hayes, who works with both victims and perpetrators of sexual violence, added: *"Your feelings are what they are."* Hayes said he believes that instructing the victim to forgive the offender in the beginning puts an additional burden on the victim.

Within this chapter, I have included some comments from Dr. William Tyson, a North Carolina psychologist. He adds that forgiveness *"means only that we don't condemn. You don't have to forgive anyone who has not said they are sorry yet.*

"Acknowledging what has happened and that the offenders' actions were theirs alone and that turning them in was the right thing," is an important requirement when it comes to treating offenders, according to Tyson. It is also important for the victim. *"Forgiveness is a lack of condemnation. It does not mean that what the person (offender) did is okay and that he does not have to pay for it,"* Tyson said.

Forgiving the offender as an avenue of finding relief from the impact of sexual abuse is emphasized by biblical leaders. It is seen as an important step of healing. *"Some people would not agree with me,"* said Rev. Charles Steven Rosser of North Carolina during an interview with me a few years ago, *"but it is not a matter of looking at a person's degree. The counselor has to deal with the soul of a person.*

"Scripture says we are spirit, soul and body. The soul is that part of us that is our mind, as well as our emotions. If you only address the

soul ... not the spirit part of the person, then there is not a complete healing. The drugs that some doctors may use for patients seeking to heal themselves of the emotional burdens of sexual abuse essentially cause the victim to become anesthetized, and then they are not really dealing with their problem. You have to treat the cause not just the symptom," Rosser said.

"There is forgiveness," Rosser pointed out. "There is grace, simple and to the point. There is no condemnation for those who seek Jesus Christ. The victim has to recognize that the person who did this to them is not well," Rosser continued.

"The child molester or pedophile is in sin. Sin is not a relative thing. Sin does not just affect the victim. It affects family members, for example. I believe in treatment ... But in our natural reasoning, we have a sense of justice. When something violates it, we tend to think we are justified for the anger. They took something from us ... our innocence or virginity. A child molester action's are repulsive. Here is a person who is in need of healing. A person who has been a victim of such a person has to understand we are all capable of sin and in need of forgiveness.

" 'For if you forgive men not of their trespasses, neither will you be forgiven.' (Matthew 6:15). All of us have sinned. We have a tendency to put degrees on certain sins. Some say murder, for example, is worse than stealing a candy bar, but the root is still the same.

"... When you feed a perversion, it will get a hold of you ... then you start to feed upon it, and it is no longer a fantasy, but an obsession ... The whole point I would like to make about sexual abuse is that when there is a breakdown in looking at the Word of God, then there is a breakdown in listening to it."

California Episcopalian priest Father Craig Lister also agreed to speak with me during the initial research stages of writing this book. I have included some of his thoughts on forgiveness too. Lister holds similar views, but added: *"In the Christian faith, Christ came to bring wholeness to people. The greatest manifestation or proof of it, is all the healing miracles that you see in the Bible. More important than physical healing, Christ brought wholeness to people's lives, and most important, spiritual wholeness. Someone who has been molested as a child has suffered physical injury, which heals pretty fast, and emotional injury, which takes more time to get over. I think that such a person suffers spiritual injury. Victims of sexual abuse may have real concerns about their own sense of self-worth and feel themselves to be more vulnerable generally than other people.*

"...The scriptures condemn anything that we consider deviant sexual behavior from incest to homosexuality and so forth. Given the physical, emotional and spiritual injuries that sexual abuse inflicts on a person, we can safely say the scriptures are against this sort of thing."

In regard to therapy for adult survivors of sexual abuse, Dr. Barbara Boat, an Ohio psychologist, said that a therapist has to help the adult deal with the child within him or herself. *"Often what is good for the child is good for the adult, because in essence you are dealing with the child in the adult."*

"Accountability," said North Carolina psychologist Mark Everson, *"is where some religious approaches fall short. I believe that forgiveness is one of the important steps. Some people never reach it. There are two different types of forgiveness: the forgiveness of the perpetrator and the forgiveness of yourself."*

"The idea of forgiveness is important to a lot of people," added Boat. *"Forgiveness of the self is the hardest."*

For survivors, forgiveness is an eminent, crucial and consequential issue. Forgiveness for the offender and self and others who never tried to rescue or comfort the victim frees survivors from hate issues and allows them to move on with their lives.

Forgiveness And The Offender

For offenders out of denial, as well as for some victims, the issue of forgiveness can become a formidable obstacle on the road to doctoring wounds. The offender, I believe, spiritually wounds himself or herself with every sexual crime committed and even if and when only contemplated. During an interview with Lister, I noted several of his comments about forgiveness in regard to offenders and have included them in this section of the book.

"I would counsel an offender to find his own forgiveness in confessing his sin," he said. "...In our tradition in the church, it has been the practice of confessing one's sins to a priest. In cases like this, where the penitent can be assured his confession is not going to go any further, there is a cleansing kind of experience (in confession and absolution). God forgives people of any crime even though there may be a debt to pay society. One can do that confident of the idea that in God's eyes he is redeemed and forgiven. A lot of that comes easier if a person is able to confess his sin to another forgiven human being who can assure him of God's pardon, and also assure him of confidentiality within the context of the relationship.

"I would counsel someone who has sexually offended to seek psychiatric help. I would hope he would take full advantage of the God-given reasons and gifts that provide modern treatment for people," Lister continued. "I also think he would need to look at himself spiritually. It would not be a matter of just coming to know his forgiveness -- but to understand that God has the power to help him through this problem and put it behind him.

"This goes back to the issue of wholeness. People who are whole do not do these things. It is people who are broken and fragmented by life; though that's not to say it is only external influences that cause someone to exhibit this kind of behavior. God forgives the inner things, as well as, the external causes for such behavior.

"I have found in all conflicts between people there is always a lack of understanding. I am not saying that if there were no misunderstandings, there would be no conflicts. Understanding another person's position or circumstances is always a big help to being able to communicate and bring about acceptance. As the old saying goes, 'You may abhor the sin, but love the sinner.'

"Child molestation is a hateful violent thing. It offends our sensibilities greatly because it is done on that portion of society we see as helpless and innocent. Some child molesters were molested as children. This is not something they set out to do. When I asked my son's first-grade classmates what they wanted to do when they grew up, not one ever said he wanted to grow up to be a child molester! But, I am saying that people are responsible for their actions.

"*Society has a right to police against such incidents and punish those who commit them. If the punishment, however, is such that it makes people worse, I do not see that as helpful. If society has no interest in understanding why people do such things, then society is simply condemning itself to live with the problem forever. Maybe this is what will happen.*

"*I suspect one way to begin healing the sex offender is having someone understand him and having the victimizer believe he is understood. When you stop and look into people's pasts, you wonder how they are as normal as they are. Some parents do cruel things. I am sure these things have powerful effects on people later on.*"

Another thing Lister emphasized is that an offender must be genuinely interested in getting help before he can be helped. "*I am a vulnerable counselor. If someone is going to trick me it is not hard. If someone is going to be insincere, I am not going to know it necessarily. I feel bad about that. But in the long run, the person with the problem is just dumping it back in his own lap.*

"*My job as a clergyman is to listen and witness to God's love ... Any therapy I can offer is limited to being caring and supportive, and hope influences such as these help people understand how much God loves them whether or not they have molested people. Perhaps a clergyman's efforts would light a spark that would lead them to recovery.*"

To Lister's comments, psychologist Tyson added in a later interview: "*Confession needs to be followed by repentance and atonement. Recovery must include a willingness to embrace the legal and social consequences. Forgiveness is a gift. It should not be coerced or negotiated like a business contract.*"

Prevention Strategies

One study estimated that 30 to 46 percent of all children in the United States will be sexually assaulted before they are 18 years old, according to "*THE KEY TO HAVING FUN IS BEING SAFE, TEACHING PERSONAL SAFETY TO CHILDREN,*" a pamphlet, written and published by Flora Colao and Tamar Hosansky.* Sexual abuse can be prevented with proper guidance from parents and/or caregivers. Children need specific examples of potentially dangerous situations. Simply telling your child never to talk with strangers is not enough. (See prevention checklist at the end of this chapter for more on strangers.) A parent or guardian may elect to take this approach:

"Someone might try to touch you in a way that you don't like ... kiss you when you don't want to ... show you their naked body ... ask you to undress in front of them ... ask you to go someplace with them." *
{ Source: "*THE KEY TO HAVING FUN IS BEING SAFE, TEACHING PERSONAL SAFETY TO CHILDREN,*" **a pamphlet, by Flora Colao and Tamar Hosansky. Copyright (c) 1982, 1983, 1987. All Rights Reserved. Reprinted with permission. }**

When children are taught to be aware of potentially dangerous situations and the lures offenders might use, children will trust themselves and their instincts to fight back or run away from an offender and tell an authoritative figure about the situation or what they feared or what was suggested. When children are esteemed by the willingness of parents, caretakers, legal guardians, teachers and physicians to instruct them on the properness of protecting oneself from abuse, children are reminded how much they are loved and cherished. They are shown a dignified way of loving themselves. This emphasizes a child's worthiness of being loved by empowering them to stop abuse before it occurs. Another important point is that children should be taught it is okay to say, "*No*." Teaching a child not to say, "*No*" and that doing so is rude, leaves him or her open and vulnerable or makes an easy prey for a pedophile, for example. (Children are entitled to their own feelings.)

In "*THE KEY TO HAVING FUN IS BEING SAFE*," safety tips include advocations to bite and hit, scream, yell, make a scene, run away, question authority, lie or not answer questions and the right to privacy. According to the pamphlet:

"A common strategy attackers use with children is to ask seemingly innocent questions. Children need to know that it's okay for them to say: their parents are home, *even when they really aren't* ... Some attackers try to con children by saying things like 'Your mother said I should take you home, -- check in on you, etc." Children need to know that it's okay to say, 'I don't believe you' ... Often attackers rely on a child's compliance. Sometimes a loud yell will startle an attacker, or a scene (screaming, crying, kicking, attempts at running away) will alert others that something is wrong ... In some cases a child may have no other option but physical resistance. Children are natural fighters and can be taught to focus on vulnerable areas: kicking knees or shins, poking eyes, biting.

"... One way to help children prevent sexual assault is to encourage them to develop a sense of physical integrity. A sense that they have a right to their own body space and privacy. Just as we allow them to close the door when they use the bathroom, we must also allow them to say no to any unwanted physical affection and touch. Such a situation might take place: Grandma wants a kiss good-bye. *Child:* I don't want to. *Grandma:* Just one kiss. Don't you love me? *Mother to Grandma:* She's not in the mood to kiss you right now. *Mother to Child:* Would you like to throw Grandma a kiss or shake her hand?" *

{ Source: "*THE KEY TO HAVING FUN IS BEING SAFE, TEACHING PERSONAL SAFETY TO CHILDREN*," a pamphlet, by Flora Colao and Tamar Hosansky. Copyright (c) 1982, 1983, 1987. All Rights Reserved. Reprinted with permission. }

Although privacy, the right to say, '*I don't want to be touched*,' and the right to fight back are important, warning children of potential dangers cannot be stressed enough.

Educating yourself and your children about the existence and dangers of sexual abuse is one avenue of prevention. If parents and caretakers recognized patterns of sexual abuse before they got out of hand, deficiencies or potential problems could be corrected and sexual abuse prevented.

Everyone of us accesses our childhood experiences to get us through the stresses of our adult years. When and if our childhoods have been stolen by offenders and replaced with abuse-related memories, the strengths we might have otherwise put towards propelling us through the joys of life or towards solving problems unrelated to abuse issues are redirected and sometimes permanently erased. Victims who had no armor -- no shield to divide them from dysfunctional attempts of offenders seeking acceptance, submission, total control in helpless children, are abandoned without even a sword! Even if a sword is left, it is disabled -- slicing only the air and anger. Everyone loses the potentials of people who might have contributed much to the progress of humanity had the innocence of those victimized not been bombarded with oftentimes suppressed, disguised and hidden internal emotional chaos. If we remain only sympathetic -- standing on the sidelines; sometimes passively objecting when it is socially or emotionally safe, what will become of our society in the end?

The topic of sexual abuse directed itself many times (during my research and writing) towards understanding offenders. You might ask yourself, "*What's there to understand about wrongful behavior? Wrong is wrong. Period.*" By understanding the offender and patterns in behavior and number of reported cases, we can learn strategies to protect our children. So, as a layperson, understanding the different kinds of sexual offenders and what this meant in terms of rendering a protection plan became important in my quest. (A more detailed discussion of this can be found later in the book.) So, to begin with, what should we know about people who sexually offend?

"For the predatory and pedophiliac molesters, we tend to see patterns emerging during adolescence," North Carolina psychologist William Tyson explained.

"Oftentimes, they will have molested a number of children by the time they are 16 or 17 years old. They are acting on their sexual aggression. There is a small core of molesters where you see the behavior emerging full strength in adolescence. In other cases, recognizing that a problem is emerging lets us know that some offenders will need to be incarcerated at an earlier age...We are able to see a predatory pattern in some young offenders. They are just going to keep doing it."

Recognizing who potential child molesters are is part of educating yourself about sexual abuse. *"The problem with the sexual offender profile is that such profiles are potentially misleading,"* Tyson said. *"For a long time, we thought that child molesters were kind of greasy-looking fellows who drove around your neighborhood and said, 'Shiny nickel, little girl?' In fact, child molesters are often the most trusted person in your life. The problem with child molester profiles is that they make us look for a certain type of person instead of making us recognize that just about anybody could be a child molester, "* he continued.

"The reality is that anybody can molest a child. There are not specific psychological or sociological categories of people who do this. There is a broad range of people who molest children. You have to be prepared from wherever it comes from; and from wherever it comes from, you are going to be surprised. The only classification scheme for child molesters I will buy is: 'Whoever you

don't expect.' When you say, 'Oh, it could not possibly be him. I would never believe he would molest a child.'

"A lot of molesters thought they would never molest a child until it was too late," Tyson said. "A lot of child molesters dissociate from their actions because they do not believe they did it. They do not want to believe they are one of those people who would molest a child," he continued. "If you see someone who has been drinking and using a lot of drugs," Tyson warned, "someone who has deteriorated in a variety of areas in his life and is left alone with children, there is a good chance he is going to molest them."

Good courses in sex education in early adolescence could go miles in preventing sexual abuse, according to Tyson. "*There are many individual child molesters who do not know that their behavior is wrong and damaging,*" Tyson said. "*They have grown up with it. They learned about sex on the street or from pornography. They simply do not understand the impact of their sexual behavior ... I am not talking about these fairy tale courses in sex education. We need courses on what sex is really about -- courses that teach what the real world of sexual behavior is about in clear and straight language that would address the problem of child molestation being wrong and damaging. They should point out that it is a criminal offense.*"

Tyson said that much of the sex education for teenagers is inadequate. "*It's an emotional topic. If you dared talk about this in schools, you would be crucified. People would raise hell about it. But without education, people are immobilized when they are presented with the situation ...*

"*The sex offender starts with touching. It's a progression. Today, we are getting more and more cases where children report after one or two incidences of touching rather than waiting until it gets worse. I think this has come about as a result of educating children more. It is now the acceptable thing to do, whereas ten years ago, the child did not know what to do. By the time a child told (10 years ago), it was because he was in such distress he was coming apart at the seams."*

One way of preventing sexual abuse is to stop sexual ignorance. *"Some child molesters know what they are doing is wrong in theory -- but they know it like they know a lot of rules,"* Tyson said. *"Some have nothing to compare their actions to except other forms of violence or similar incidences. Had some seen a film, for example, on the dangers of sexual abuse, they might have had something to compare it to. Bringing sex out of the dark and making it something other than a naughty experience, allows you to discriminate as to what is wrong and what is right."*

In regard to preventing child molestation, therapist Hayes had this to add: *"People say that if you are molested, 'this' is what you are supposed to do, but they don't tell potential molesters that you should not do it or how to avoid doing it. And despite these things, we don't do much to teach children how to avoid it.*

"We assume that people know something is wrong because it against the law, or that they will not do it simply because it is illegal. The truth is people who molest children are masters of rationalization and denial. They are quite easily able to convince themselves that their actions are both acceptable and non-harmful."

Defense Strategies That Reinforce Prevention

All children should be taught how to use telephones -- how to call for help: 911 (the police). They should also be taught as soon as they are capable: their home telephone number and area code, their full names, parents' full names, their address, the names of their hometown and state, the full names of any significant caretakers and their telephone numbers. They should be informed that pay phones do not require money for 911 (emergency) calls. Instructing a child on how to use a pay phone is a good idea too.

They should be gently told that it is okay to report offenders or would-be offenders or even their peers if threatened by them with any action that makes the child feel uncomfortable. Some childhood victims of sexual abuse may act out what has been done to them on other children. (See *Chapter IV: What Are The Signs Of Sexual Abuse?* for more information.)

In addition to education and counselors, parents can take steps in preventing the likelihood of sexual assault by thoroughly checking references of potential nannies or baby-sitters. Requiring and checking references as far back as possible may give parents more accurate information when deciding upon a baby-sitter.

Visiting a potential baby-sitter's house and family may also help parents to make wiser decisions when hiring a baby-sitter. Requiring personal/character, as well as, business/professional references could be helpful. Parents should obligate themselves extensively to thoroughly checking personal and professional references of baby-sitter applicants. Do not allow your personal business and career ambitions to interfere with the obligations to your children in spending the extra time needed to find an appropriate caretaker.

Do not be fooled by a few good references and a friendly face. You should check to see if the person who wants the nanny or baby-sitter position has a criminal record. This can be done by checking public documents at your local courthouse or at the courthouse in the towns the applicant has lived in.

Plan two or three days to have potential long-term nannies

baby-sit your children while you are in the house -- within visual and hearing range to see how they work or socialize or interact with your children. Of course, a potential offender or habitual offender is not going to offend in front of you; however, having a baby-sitter work in front of you will give you better insight into their personality and allow you time to observe them in action and/or reconsider your decision or discuss your concerns with the sitter. If you do not feel completely at ease with a potential nanny, keep looking.

It is important to always ask your children how they feel about a potential sitter or even a sitter they may have had for years. If a teenager is hired or considered for a baby-sitter task or position, speak with the applicant's parents; ask for, obtain and call all references; ask about school performance and interests. Get to know them, so you can determine if they are worthy of passing through your doorway.

Making your requirements and even fears well-known to applicants in the beginning might frighten off a potential or practicing molester from pursuing the nanny or baby-sitter position, and thus make narrowing down your choices easier.

Parents should also be aware of and request information on any other person who might be assisting the main baby-sitter -- the baby-sitter's spouse, baby-sitter's relatives, their neighbor or your neighbor. Offenders often seek out situations that give them access to children. For instance, offenders may court and marry women with children and women who baby-sit other people's children.

Offenders have been known to pursue careers and social activities that give them access to children. These include Cub and Boy scout leaders, youth group leaders, football, baseball, and basketball coaches, school teachers, school counselors, special education teachers, caretakers, and baby-sitters, among others.

Offenders look for opportunities to gain access to children in everyday places such as malls, shopping centers, parks, playgrounds, school yards, and neighborhood roads and streets. Offenders look for opportunities that reveal a child is not being protected -- watched closely and cared for by responsible adults. They look for children in situations where parents are preoccupied with careers and work and in situations or circumstances that reveal a child in need of attention or a child who is not attended to closely emotionally or physically. They look for children who may not be looked out for at all times.

Visiting your child's school periodically and getting to know each of his or her teachers is a good habit to practice, but it might also help you in the event you suspect your child has been or is being abused. It is imperative that you know the adults and young teens your child is socializing with: coaches, choir directors, church group leaders for young people's social activities, club leaders and directors for girl and boy scouts. Making yourself known as a concerned parent to all these people may deter a potential molester from making any attempts to sexually assault your child.

Remember that the sexual abuser uses the abuse he or she inflicts on a child or children to coax victims into secrecy and feelings of shame -- shame the offenders should feel.

Prevention Checklist For Chapter I

Details of mapping out a personal plan to prevent sexual abuse will vary, depending on whether you are a parent, teacher, caretaker, single with no children, grandparent, aunt, uncle, legislator, physician, etc.; however, some of the suggestions listed in this chapter can be used no matter who you are. Possible solutions to prevent abuse could include some or all of the following:

__ Contact organizations listed at the end of this chapter for additional information about child sexual assault.

__ Read to your children books on child abuse prevention that are geared to children. One such book for children is titled: *It's Okay to Say Don't, A Book About Protecting Yourself* by Betty Beogehold. It is suitable for children. (Check with your local libraries and book stores for appropriate books.)

__ Read books to children that emphasize correct, proper, and acceptable behaviors in general. Some excellent children's books include Joy Berry's "LET'S TALK ABOUT" series: *SAYING NO, NEEDING ATTENTION, FEELING ANGRY, FEELING AFRAID, FEELING SAD, BEING HELPFUL*. There are many other children's books that instruct children on social limitations while boosting self-esteem, so check with your local library and book stores. Remember that it is *not* necessary to talk about "*sex*" in order to esteem and empower children to protect themselves from sexual abuse. Children who possess healthy self-regards and understand that social rules apply to everyone do not make easy prey for offenders.

__ Instruct children on the old rule of not talking to strangers. It is still an important lesson in protection. A video, *The Berenstain*

Bears: Learn About Strangers, is a non-threatening approach to child protection in general. It is wise to not put children at more risk by telling them not to talk to any strangers. Children need to understand which strangers would be okay to ask for help in the event they became lost or were abducted. Uniformed police officers, security guards in a mall, mothers or fathers with children, and/or babies, sales clerks, and store owners are the kinds of strangers children can be taught to distinguish from others in the event of an emergency. Children can be taught how to ask for proper identification from people identifying themselves as police and security officers. Children can also be taught to run away from people who refuse to allow proper identification verification by calling 911 or the police station.

___ Thoroughly check all references of potential baby-sitters and people who are to be entrusted with caring for your child or children.

___ Thoroughly check for possible criminal records (at your local courthouse) of all potential nannies and anyone who might be assisting the nanny.

___ Share your concerns about prevention with teachers and those involved in caring for and teaching your child.

___ Create an emotionally safe home environment that promotes acceptance and freedom to express oneself. Praise your child or children for accomplishments, even the smallest achievements and spend time talking and doing things together -- visiting parks, museums, playing.

___ Read about and implement ways to increase a child's self-esteem. Share what you decide to use in regard to building esteem, a healthy self-regard, with your child's or children's caretakers, teachers, grandparents. (*How to Develop Self-Esteem*

In Your Child: 6 Vital Ingredients by Bettie B. Youngs, Ph.D, Ed.D and *YOUR CHILD'S SELF-ESTEEM* by Dorothy Corkille Briggs are good reading sources for parents and caretakers for this task.)

___ Educate yourself about what sexual abuse is and how to prevent it by reading this book and others. (Refer to the list of references in the back of this book for additional reading sources.)

___ Teach children as soon as they are capable their full names, parents' full names, addresses, telephone numbers, names of their hometowns and states, how to use a telephone, public or booth phone, even car phones and how to call 911 or the police or operator for help.

___ Keep a careful lookout for your child's whereabouts at all times -- especially in public parks, restrooms, while visiting friends and relatives, stores, churches, museums, malls, etc. Avoid allowing your children to use public restrooms without being accompanied by a parent or guardian.

___ Teach children that no matter who has been entrusted with their care and protection, no one is allowed to cross certain boundaries -- not relatives, parents, friends, no one. Teach children that no one is allowed to touch areas that their bathing suits or underclothing regularly cover.

___ Nurture and instill the importance of honesty and trust in your children. Be knowledgeable of potential catch-22 situations that could trap a child into low self-esteem, fear and secrecy.

___ Model socially acceptable behavior.

___ Keep a caring lookout for the safety of children you see playing on playgrounds, in parks, on city streets, in neighborhoods, countrysides, malls, school grounds, etc. and be prepared to report any suspicions to the police and social services departments in your area.

___ Teach children about never going anywhere with a stranger who just happens to know their name or the names of their parents.

___ Write editorials that comment on the suitability of certain children's programs, cartoons, movies, books, magazines, etc.

___ Write letters promoting awareness of sexual abuse prevention to public officials, school officials and the media.

___ Voice the importance of preventing child sexual abuse and other forms of child abuse to your friends and relatives.

___ Use child sexual abuse prevention techniques mentioned in this chapter, as well as, in other chapters of this book.

___ Support or introduce into junior and high schools sex education classes that implement lessons and discussions on what is not socially acceptable sexual behavior. These classes should also include information on penalties for sexually deviant behavior and potential outcomes for victims, survivors and offenders.

___ Remind yourself frequently of the importance of a healthy childhood -- one devoid of violence, sexual deviance.

___ Reassess your parenting techniques in regard to instilling good self-esteem and self-discipline in your child or children. Remember that a child who has been sexually abused or just approached by an offender with suggestions is not going to want to confide the offense in someone who might beat them or accuse them of lying. This further entraps an abused child into secrecy about being assaulted and puts them at more risks for additional harm. Children with healthy self-esteems will be more likely to stand up for themselves in the face of potential sexual abuse; thus, empowering them to prevent it from occurring.

Alternatives to spanking most always work the best, and they include: Childproofing your home to avoid entire situations that not doing so would render; defusing potentially sticky situations by introducing humor; cleverly introducing distractions; using gentle, but informative age-appropriate warnings of danger, and emphasizing the importance of safety, etc.; withdrawing privileges; using time-out (one minute of time-out for each year of the child's age); pointing out and praising good behavior; constructive discussion with explanations for why certain behaviors are unacceptable, reading books with themes portraying acceptable and good behavior to children.

Requiring older children to write an essay on why any given behavior was wrong is another possible substitute to spanking.

Remember that offenders prey on children who demonstrate over-compliance and those whose esteems are not geared to protecting themselves by shouting, "No!" and running away or causing a scene. Children with high self-regard will not be overwhelmed with having to obey an order or even a suggestion, physical or verbal, from an adult.

__ Teach children that certain circumstances may require them to bite, kick, scream, shout, make a scene in public or behind closed doors to free themselves from anyone who tries to trick or coerce them. Teach children what they need to know to free themselves from anyone who might force them into doing something they would not normally do or from anyone who tries to do something to them that would cause them to feel strange or frightened or hurt.

___ Report all suspicions of sexual abuse to the police and social services departments in your area, and provide as many details about the report as you are able. If you are nervous about reporting your suspicions, write everything you suspect down on paper and have it handy when you call the child protective division at the county social services department. Contact the social services department in the area where you believe the child lives. Anyone who makes a report with all good intentions is immune from civil and/or criminal liabilities.

You should report your suspicions as quickly as possible, remembering that the sooner you report, the faster the authorities can stop the abuse if it in fact is occurring. You should provide the name and age of the child you suspect as being abused. You should provide the name and address of the parent or guardian legally responsible for the child. You should also provide details about suspected injuries and any other information that might be helpful. If you witness the abuse and do not have names, provide the name of the location where you witnessed the crime and descriptions, approximate ages of the persons involved and a license plate number may prove helpful. A report does not mean "*fact;*" however, failing to report could destroy the life of an innocent.

Chapter I Checklist Summary For Adult Survivors

___ Prayer

___ Understand the abuse was not your fault.

__ Read about child sexual abuse and the experiences of other survivors.

__ Journal your thoughts about your abuse experiences. (To keep your privacy, you may decide to destroy it later.)

__ Obtain counseling from a counselor specializing in helping adult survivors of child sexual abuse. Share your experiences with a minister or close friend.

There are also organizations devoted to information on child sexual abuse and the prevention of it. I have listed some of these here.

NATIONAL ORGANIZATIONS LIST FOR INFORMATION:

1) CHILDREN'S SAFETY PROJECT
   GREENWICH HOUSE, INC.
   27 BARROW STREET
   NEW YORK, N.Y. 10014
   (212) 924-1091
   (212) 242-4140 FAX: (212) 366-4226

2) CHILDHELP USA
   P.O. BOX 630
   LOS ANGELES, CA. 90028

   NATIONAL CHILD ABUSE HOTLINE:
   1-800-4A CHILD (422-4453)

   NOTE: COUNSELORS ARE ALWAYS AVAILABLE TO DIRECT CALLERS FROM ANY STATE TO LOCAL

44

SOURCES OF HELP.

*3) NATIONAL CLEARINGHOUSE ON CHILD ABUSE
AND NEGLECT INFORMATION: P.O.
BOX 1182, WASHINGTON. D.C. 20013*

*1 (800) 394-3366,
1-800-FYI-3366.*

*NOTE: THIS CLEARINGHOUSE IS MANAGED BY THE NATIONAL
CENTER ON CHILD ABUSE AND NEGLECT. IT PROVIDES
INFORMATION ON RESEARCH, CURRENT ISSUES, PROGRAMS
AND LEGISLATION RELATED TO ABUSE AND NEGLECT.*

*The National Clearinghouse on Child Abuse and Neglect is a
national resource for professionals and concerned citizens seeking
information on the prevention, identification and treatment of child
abuse and neglect. Its mission includes collecting, storing,
organizing and disseminating information on all aspects of child
maltreatment. This information includes: policy and legislation,
identification and investigation, treatment, prevention, research,
grant activities, public awareness, training and education, public
and private programs in regard to child maltreatment. The
Clearinghouse also is responsible for promoting cooperation among
the many organizations working to end child maltreatment.*

*4) AMERICAN HUMANE ASSOCIATION
63 INVERNESS DRIVE EAST
ENGLEWOOD, CO. 80112-5117
Children's Division: (303) 792-9900
FAX: 303-792-5333*

*The American Humane Association provides all sorts of free
information about preventing sexual abuse, as well as, other
information regarding child abuse and neglect.*

CHAPTER

"No one is to approach any close relative to have sexual relations ... " -- **Leviticus 18:06.** *(NIV)*.

Individual Recollections From Adult Survivors

To Cope And Heal / Or Cope And Fester

In order to talk about prevention, it may be interesting for you to understand the long term implications of what we need to prevent. Of course, sexual abuse stories are difficult to think about, and my assumption in this chapter is that you are reading this book for understanding -- not sensationalism. You are reading for information, answers and validation of the current serious threat sexual abuse poses for our children and our society.

You may have been victimized yourself or have a friend or family member who may have been sexually abused. You might be a teacher, social services agent, nurse, physician or a parent, concerned aunt, uncle.

Chapters I and IV provide much in terms of understanding what to look for when sexual abuse is suspected and how to go about preventing sexual abuse from ever occurring or stopping it from continuing once it has been witnessed or reported.

This chapter, however, offers a deeper understanding because it contains the stories, thoughts and conclusions about individual sexual abuse situations from real people -- adults who suffered as children. These adults were denied the God-given right to grow up in emotionally and physically safe environments -- devoid of the pedophile's selfish, narcissistic, haughty and demented offenses.

Individual accounts of sexual abuse experiences in this chapter are sad and shocking. If we look closely enough, we find that children who are victimized look for ways within their individual capabilities and environmental leeways to remove themselves from sexual abuse situations -- emotionally and physically. They look for ways out and for ways to cope. In each interview, you will discover what this means or meant for survivors. Coping for some leads to drug and alcohol abuse, sexual promiscuity or feelings and actions to isolate oneself from others.

The survivors in this chapter dealt with the intrusions of their offenders with the varying tools and skills their dysfunctional environments rendered. Most of the survivors survived in atmospheres that embodied the silent watchful eyes of opportunity seekers, the offenders. This chapter, in particular, is not intended reading for children, and the irony here is that we are discussing children.

The stories reflect irreparable emotional damage at first glance, but as you sympathize with their circumstances, it will become apparent that their words are stepping stones to relief -- relief in finally being able to fight their intruders and relief that maybe today as you read, you will be motivated to hinder the continuance of sexual abuse and understand fully what we are fighting, and develop your own personal plan for prevention from ideas presented in this book.

We are fighting fear. We are battling for the sharpest pair of scissors to cut the common threads of helplessness, shame and anger -- common consequences for survivors. We want to ungag mouths and resuscitate some dignity back into the lives of survivors whose childhoods drowned in silence. We want to empower our children and ourselves with information and then put a plan to prevent into action.

Survivor stories are indisputable reflections of truth. They are indisputable when we understand that children do not lie about having been sexually abused; nor do adult survivors. When survivors tell, it is an attempt to debride their childhood wounds that have festered into adulthood. As you read these accounts, try to imagine these survivors as children telling you as a confidant. If you are a survivor, these stories will convince you that you are not suffering alone.

If you are a concerned citizen trying to learn more about sexual abuse, the true accounts in this chapter will sensitize you to this social and familial problem that hides in fears and shame for victims and in the lies and delusions of the pedophile. Survivors feel as if they are confessing to a crime because they are socialized by the offender to believe the assaults are their fault.

You will discover that telling the worst part for survivors varies with sexual abuse experiences, and understand that the worst part of child sexual abuse is that its destructive journey has been licentious and undisturbed due to our indifference and detachment.

Prevention will disarm the monsters survivors experience as depression, sleeping problems, thoughts of and attempts at suicide, listlessness, senses of drifting through life without any goals and feelings of isolation or being different from other adults; self-destructive behavior -- anorexia, bulimia, overeating, alcohol and drug abuse, prostitution; troubled and/or abusive relationships with spouses, boyfriends or girlfriends.

Panic attacks, feelings of stigmatization and alienation, mistrust, low self-esteem, anxiety, and an increased worry about the safety of others are difficult battles for some survivors too. Prevention will rid us of the socially and emotionally destructive "victim role" played out in the lives of the sexually abused until or unless they find a way to break the cycle.

Although some prior victims may grow into adults who repeat the abuse, most do not repeat the sexual abuse. All adult survivors whose interviews I included in this chapter expressed disgust at the idea of anyone suggesting they might repeat the abuse. Talking about past abuse is a step in the right direction in terms of releasing pent up anger and sadness, which is often suppressed by survivors who believe others will in some way blame them for the experience or view them as marked.

One of the interviews in this chapter reveals an account where a survivor disclosed painful ordeals to an insensitive individual who caused more psychological rejection and created, for the survivor, still another obstacle. Survivors risk scorn and scapegoating when or if they ever choose to disclose their offender's actions. Their silence, however, would put more children at risk. Disbelief reactions cause more fears to rise in victims and survivors who "talk."

Individual Recollections From Adult Survivors

Three Accounts From Women Survivors Sexually Abused By Their Stepfathers

"When society breaks down, it begins to morally decay." -- Reverend Charles Steven Rosser, Abundant Life Christian Center, Sanford, North Carolina.

Homemaker's Story Of Childhood Abuse

Background:

This account is from a 26-year-old female who was sexually abused and raped by her stepfather. The sexual abuse started when she was six years old and continued until she was 12. This woman has attempted college several times, but quit because of feelings of being overwhelmed, fears of answering questions in front of a lot of people and being wrong and difficulties in concentrating.

She is currently self-employed and has never received any therapy. She is married and has no children. She suffers from endometriosis and now questions whether some of the scar formations she has could have come from the sexual abuse. The research contained here makes no medical judgments concerning her endometriosis -- only a mention of this condition because it is of concern at the original time of this writing, to the interviewee survivor. She has never told her gynecologist about the abuse -- but plans to seek therapy when she feels ready.

Presently, she has confided the abuse and rape in her mother and husband. Her biological parents are divorced. Her stepfather and mother are now divorced, and her mother has remarried. Through her honesty and sincerity, it is easy to see how the abuse she experienced damaged her self-image and her self-esteem and how she still struggles.

As she recounted her childhood history of being sexually abused, I was amazed at how matter-of-fact she appeared, not once breaking into tears. I think her heart cries silently, while her face cries selectively -- sharing only when it is emotionally safe. This is true of most survivors; certainly true of those I have interviewed and spoken with.

Her sharing is a gift to us, but it is one of warning and education. This survivor's concerns are centered on the protection of her siblings and mother and far-removed from herself. I believe her consent to interview is a reflection of her increased concern about the safety of others. Here is her story:

Recollections

"At the time of the abuse, my mother was pregnant with my younger brother. My older brother and I lived in the house. My stepfather used to beat my older brother and mother ....

"*The sexual abuse started when I was six. I do not remember the first incident. I just remember what happened down the road. My stepfather used to come up in my bedroom, and I don't know what he thought I was ... He would fondle me. He touched every part of my body that he felt like touching. He would kiss me. I used to be afraid of him. He used to come up there just about every night.*

"*It got to the point where I started asking my brother, who is two years older, to sleep on the side of the bed that was facing out, and I would sleep on the part next to the wall.*

"*Every night, when he would come in, he would wake up my brother and say, 'Go to your own room.' I would hold my brother, and tell him I was afraid and not to leave. I did not want him to leave.*

"*My brother had no idea what was going on. He just thought I was afraid .... I know he (stepfather) used to kiss me and rub my body and make me touch him. I do not remember specific time periods. When he started penetrating me, all the incidents started running together in my mind.*

"*I used to fight with my stepfather when he would molest me. I used to cry and hold on to my brother's arm to try and make my stepfather leave me be.*

"*Sometimes, he would let my brother stay with me, but my stepfather would reach over ... I would shake my brother to wake him up to see what was going on. I couldn't tell him, but I wanted him to see what was happening to me. I thought he could stop it. He was a sound sleeper. He would not wake up.*

"I probably would confront my stepfather now about what he did, but I would not know what to say to him at this point. He is so mentally far gone.

"He was married before he married my mother, and he shot his first wife in the leg because she was not doing what he said. He married my mother and beat her up. We used to live on a farm. My stepfather would beat my brother with a leather strap and saddle stirrups. My brother had big red welts up and down his legs.

"Now, my brother is older, he may have put everything together, but if he has, he has never said anything to me about it.

"Why my mother let these things go on, I do not know. Because I love her, I try to justify her actions. The only reason I can see for her allowing him to do this to me is that she was so frightened of him. She was probably afraid of being beaten for confronting him with it. Rather than her being beaten, she sacrificed me.

"I never told her about what happened to me until she asked me. She was the one who asked me about it, so she must have known he was doing this to me.

"My personal opinion about this is that my mother needs to see a therapist. My mother is fifty years old. An uncle sexually abused her when she was five years old. She said she never told anyone because this uncle was very wealthy and respected by our family. He was like an idol in our family, and no one would have believed her had she told. So, she never told anybody except me on the day she asked me had I been molested. She told me not to worry about it. She said, 'I was too when I was five.'

"I think this attitude is pitiful. I do not think it is okay to say because it happened to me it is okay for it to happen to other kids ....

What She Remembers About The Abuse:

"I do not remember the exact time frame ... he would make me lay in bed with him. My stepfather would make me kiss him, and he would touch me.

"As I started getting older, he started making me touch him with my hands and orally. I don't know exactly -- but I was probably ten or eleven years old then. This is also when he started forcing me to have intercourse with him ....

"I have never considered him my parent. He is my stepfather. Please never refer to him as my parent (nervous laughter). He is the father of my younger brother and sister, and they have not seen him since my mother divorced him ....

"When it (the sexual abuse and rapes) was (were) happening to me, I had absolutely no idea what was going on. When I was six years old, it was something that you never heard of on television.

"Now, society has ads and programs on television about it, so that children can find out what to do if this happens to them ....

"The biggest thing that sticks out in my mind about the things that were happening to me then is ... I can see now, it was almost like he (stepfather) wanted to get caught doing it. There were days when I had my friends over, and he would call me out of the room. He would have nothing to say to me. He would start kissing and touching me and stuff.

"I can't see why he would do this. I found it embarrassing because I would have to go back into the room, where my friends were. They would ask, 'What did he want?' There was nothing I could say to them. He used to do that a lot ... even when his friends were over. During these times he called me out of the room ... and made me start touching him.

"Now, I do not think I have anything to say to him. I think that people like him should be shot. I think that people like him need some kind of therapy.

" .... When he was not drinking, which were very few days, he was perfect to be around. But when he was drinking and smoking pot, I could not stand to be around him. He felt like he had to be in control of everyone else's life. He would beat my mother. He would beat my brother. For some reason rather than beating me, he found sexually abusing me as controlling in my life.

"Everything he did to me was sexual. He never really beat me .... When my mother was pregnant with my little brother, my stepfather did not want her to have any other children, so he would kick her in the stomach with his cowboy boots to try to make her miscarry the baby.

"She later gave birth to my brother in the hospital and came back home ... My brother was only two years old when she got pregnant with my little sister.

"We had to move. There were times we had to leave the house in the middle of the night because my stepfather would get really mean and beat my mother. The last time we left, we had to leave the house in the middle of the night through a corn field.

"He followed us. One time we left and went to our grandmother's house. He came there banging on the doors. He started throwing rocks at the windows and breaking them out because he wanted my mother. He became very violent toward everybody. He wanted us back in his house under his reign. He had to be very controlling over everybody ....

"He must have been around thirty-seven years old when he first molested me ... I have pretty much blocked the sexual abuse out of my mind. When I was growing up I pretended it did not happen, and that it was just a nightmare.

"To this day, I do not like to be woke up in the middle of the night. When my husband would do this, I would react as if he were pushing sex on me just like my stepfather. My husband does not see it that way. He was just trying to be loving.

"Before I told my husband about the abuse, he could not understand why I would get mad at him and start yelling at him in the bed. When we got to the point where we were just about to get divorced, I told him.

"Telling my husband has helped. Having my mother know, I don't think has helped in any way. The way my mother found out was kind of strange. I was standing at the door one night, and she asked me if he had molested me, and I said , 'Yes.' My stepfather had told my mother that he hated her and that he would make her pay for it. She understood it as him making her pay through me.

"She asked me if he had molested me, and I said, 'Yes,' so I know that she knew because she said that. My stepfather is a raving maniac. I believe he has serious mental problems. After he told her that, he started buying books with little girls in them -- nude pornography that had little girls and men in it.

"My mother said there was nothing to worry about because it had happened with her and her uncle. That was the only time me and my mom have ever spoke of it.

"I told my husband about it this year. I mainly told him because we had some sexual hang-ups, which I believe all came from the sexual abuse I experienced.

"Rather than arguing constantly with my husband about sex, and for him to understand, I decided he needed to know the truth. My husband has been very supportive, but he still does not comprehend everything that I have told him.

"When I hear about things like this happening to other children now, it makes me sick! It makes me angry to think someone would do the things that were done to me as a child to another child. I even categorize sexual abuse and rape differently when it happens to a child than when it happens when you are older. At least when you are older, you are a little more mentally stable to deal with it than when you are a child."

Associations: Memory Links To The Past

"Talking about associations ... my mom is now remarried to another man. During my sister's whole life, it seems I have been terrified of the fear of this man touching her. When she was little, this man gave her a lot of attention -- not positive -- but negative attention.

"I remember a time when she was too young to be potty trained. He would slap her because she could not use the toilet. She was too young to use the toilet. Because she wore a diaper, and would go to the bathroom in her diaper, he would slap her. I remember one time sitting in my bedroom and seeing him kick her from across the hall into my bedroom. She had on a diaper.

"My sister is thirteen years younger than I am and then, she was not even one year old. "I remember he (second stepfather) would lay down with her when she took a nap. This scared me. I have never told her about me, but I have told her if he ever touched her in a manner she was not comfortable with to come and tell me, and I would take her out of the house.

"... Just recently, I visited my mother and new stepfather. I had been downstairs in my brother's old room sleeping. I woke up and found my mother sleeping on the couch. I went back into my sister's bedroom, and she was not there. I knew my stepfather was in his room sleeping. The only thing I could think of was that he had gotten my little sister and that she was in his bed. This is the only thing I could think of. I started getting panicky and paranoid. I did not know what we were going to do if she was in there. We were going to do something. I wanted everyone up.

"I went into the living room and shook my mother. I said, 'I want to know right now. Where is she?' I mean, if she was in his room, I was going to make the whole family barge in there and get her out. This is how I felt. My mom said, 'I think she is downstairs sleeping,' so I went downstairs and found her.

"As it turned out, she had been sleeping in the same bedroom with me. I had not seen her earlier because when I got up it was pitch dark. I guess I had freaked out .... He is her stepfather, and I guess I am overly protective toward her about any attention he shows her .... especially when I think he is starting to show her more attention than he should.

58

"He has never had any kids, and he has raised these kids. My sister is the daughter of the man who molested me. It could be that this stepfather is trying to be loving toward her, but I just don't look at it that way.

"If I think he is hugging her too much or asking her to go places with him too much, I become overly protective. So, you can see, I do not feel the same way my mother feels that being molested is okay because it happened to her."

Trying To Make Sense Of It All

She says: "My mother needs men too much. She is not independent. The man she is married to now has beaten up my younger brother to the point where I drove there and took both her children out of the house. I would not send them home until she finally called the police and kicked him out.

"He is now going to therapy. The courts have forced him to go to therapy. The therapist has put him on medication to help relax him and mellow him out. I think for my mother now, it is like living with a zombie.

"My first stepfather had therapy to please the courts. After it was over, he would go back to his old ways ....

"... I think that someone who has not gone through this can find ways to blame the victim when they really shouldn't. When you are at that age, how can you blame the child for not knowing what to do? Here, we have a grown man who knows better and a child who does not know how to tell someone. The child may not even know it is wrong ...

"I remember my stepfather telling me not to tell my mother because he would beat her. I did not want to put her through that. She was one of my options to tell, and I couldn't. I did not know who to tell. I did not give any hints. I acted as if it never existed ....

"Since then (the abuse), I have never had any confidence in myself. In college I would not go to class because I had to make a speech. Although my speech would have gotten me an A, I did not have the confidence to stand up in front of people. The thought of one person smirking scared me. I am very judgmental now.

"I always see the worst things in people before I get to know them. I have become less trusting of women. It seems I should be less trusting of men, but I am not. I don't know why. I am not a therapist, and I have never been to one. So, I don't know if it is fair for me to evaluate myself. It could be that my mother knew and did not say anything.

"I don't trust all men, but I trust men who tell me positive things about myself, that my hair looks nice or that my perfume is nice. Anyone who makes me feel better, I trust instantly.

"I met a man who told me everything to make me feel good. My girlfriend kept telling me, 'These are lines he is using on you.' What he was doing was making me feel good, and it turned out he was just using me. I could not see that, but my friend could.

"I constantly questioned this man. I really did not believe someone thought nice things about me. I asked him, and he said everything he said about me was true. Two months down the road, he moved. I wrote him letters, but I never received any replies. I have not heard from him since.

"When I met my husband, I found it difficult to believe he really meant all the things he said. Before I met him, half the men I dated were seeing five other people ....

"I think I have a low self-esteem, so that when men tell me nice things, it helps my esteem, and I trust them. I probably still would not be that way if I knew how to bring my self-esteem up by myself. When I am by myself, I go into a depression. I don't know how to pull myself out of it. It just takes a couple days, and then I am fine."

To See, Listen And Learn

This survivor's story was never heard before this interview, and it sadly shouted loud clues to people outside her home. It is difficult to believe that her teachers at school failed to take action that would have revealed the extent of her abuse. This survivor's self-esteem was poisoned from all directions. Teachers would certainly be sensitive to any home distractions at school that would hinder a child's concentration and self-confidence. Yet, no one stepped forward -- not even her own mother, to defend her.

A healthy self-esteem comes from how we truly feel about ourselves outside of others. It is our self-judgments of ourselves. It is clear this young beautiful woman's view of being a valued human was damaged. Her self-value was diminished through her abuse experiences; however, the extent of it could have been curtailed.

No one took action to defend her or action that would have taught her empowerment to defend herself. Even if her stepfather were ever brought to justice, the devastation he inflicted on her self-esteem -- self-value and confidence, and feelings of worthiness is unfathomable. The indifference exhibited by her teachers, doctors, school counselors, friends and relatives -- anyone who came in contact with her on a non-threatening level, gave her offender more reason to continue. Rebuilding her life and self-esteem will be a difficult task, and sadly, she can never regain her childhood!

The next account is illustrative of how the stress of sexual assault can cause survivors to block pieces of their lives out in order to cope.

Accounts Continued:

Chef's Story Of Childhood Abuse

Background:

This 31-year-old female survivor works as a chef today. She was sexually abused by her stepfather, who was an alcoholic. Her mother is now divorced from this survivor's stepfather and has since remarried. Presently, she has told one aunt, some close friends and her sister about the sexual abuse she experienced from ages 14 to 17. This survivor was 29 years old when she first disclosed the abuse to her sister. She has undergone some therapy. The perpetrator was in his 40s when he first abused her. She also says her stepfather abused her mother emotionally and verbally.

This survivor recalls voyeurism, when an adult watches a child or teenager for pure sexual gratification while the victim dresses, undresses, bathes or use the toilet. Voyeurism is difficult to prove; however, victims of this offense often notice something strange about their circumstances even when the victim is too young to understand an offender's motivations. We also learn from this interview that survivors sometimes have no memory of their childhoods until something or someone causes suppressed or blocked-out memories to resurface. (See *Chapter IV: What Are The Signs Of Sexual Abuse?*)

Recollections

"I ignored a lot of the sexual abuse. I was in a state of total denial -- no memory. I totally blocked it out. I could never understand why there were years missing from my life. I started therapy about two-and-a-half years ago. I went to a public health center because I knew I could not afford private counseling.

"I blocked out the memories of the sexual abuse, but it kept creeping into my lifestyle through the kinds of men I chose. I chose men who were a lot like how my stepfather was. He had a real problem grasping reality. His next million was always just around the corner, and he was the 'chasing-the-rainbow' type of man. I would end up choosing someone like that or either a chronic or recovering alcoholic. No men other than my stepfather ever abused me. I would never allow it to happen again...

"I remember bits and pieces prior to going to therapy, but I initially went to therapy because I was so angry all the time for no apparent reason. I would lash out. I could not understand why. I would remember little bits of flashbacks.

"Through therapy and telling my sister and being able to verbalize the abuse helped my emotional state. Having someone initially believe me helped. It helped comfort me. It helped me know that I am not imagining things, and that I was not going insane...

"I remember one vivid experience. It happened in the kitchen. There was never any rape involved -- just molestation. I can still remember and at times almost feel his hands on my breasts, kissing me. It felt like an eternity, but the incident probably lasted about five minutes.

"I think the only thing that stopped anything from going any further was my brother. The door was shut, and my brother had started coming out of his room. My stepfather stopped and turned around like nothing had happened. I was sixteen then. I had always been intimidated by him. I was so afraid. To me, I always looked at him as the type of person who could do some real physical harm if you fought back. This is the first time he had ever had any close contact with me ....

"He used to spank me every night before bed for no reason whatsoever. He spanked me until I was blistered. To this day, I cannot stand anyone coming up behind me and touching me, even when it is just a friendly pat. He did this ritualistically.

"I remember my mother and stepfather having arguments. She had no control over him. I told my real father what my stepfather had done -- the sexual and physical abuse. I told my father last year. He believed me. All he could say was, 'I am so sorry.'

"I was afraid to tell anyone because I did not feel anyone would believe me .... We all had separate bedrooms with locks on the doors. Being a developing teenager and obviously very self-conscious about my own body, I would go into my room and lock the door to change. My stepfather had a key. He would open the door and make me change in front of him. I would scream, 'Get out of my room! Get out of my room!' This was during my teenage years. He would laugh at me. He would say, 'This is my house. I paid for this house. I will do whatever I want.' My mother never saw him do this. She was out a lot. She worked nights ....

"After the incident in the kitchen, my mother and father got divorced, and you never saw a happier seventeen year old when that man moved out of that house ... I had very little contact with him after that time.

"My stepfather was a very touchy kind of person. Sometimes, the touches would get real uncomfortable even though nothing was happening that I can remember. A lot of it I still don't remember.

"I keep thinking there was oral sex involved, but I don't have a specific memory of it. There is no real memory. I can't explain it. The only kind of memory I have is almost in the form of a flashback .... I remember gagging. I remember a gagging sensation with it..."

Associations: Memory Links To The Past

"To this day, I do not like anything covering my neck. I feel like I am choking. I don't like turtleneck sweaters or choker-type necklaces around my neck...

"There are certain mannerisms that remind me of the abuse. I went out with a date. My date wore a suit like the kind of suits my stepfather used to wear -- dark blue business suits. I asked him what he did, and he said he was a business consultant. This is what my stepfather did for a living. I never saw this particular date again. I never went out with him again. It was just too uncomfortable ....

Therapy Helps

"The memories I have are like little flicks, not real memories, but pieces and feelings and emotions I get for almost no apparent reason ....

"The last time I had therapy was this year in January or February. I stopped therapy because my best friend died of AIDS and my brother-in-law had been diagnosed with liver cancer. They both passed away within three weeks of each other ...

"I just had to stop and chill out for a while. It was too much grieving to deal with at one time. The therapy probably would have helped, but there was just so much going on with my job, classes and everything.

"The one thing that has really helped me ... I went to a support group for adult survivors of childhood sexual abuse. It was local and sponsored by a hospital and held at a women's center .... It was group therapy. Everyone there understood what you were talking about; however, there were a few there who were still very real victims."

Memories She Would Like To Forget

"We had a pool, and he (stepfather) used to make us (siblings) skinny dip. I remember it was real hot, and I went out swimming. I remember him standing at the window. I was outside. While he watched, his legs were apart. I was swimming and diving, and he was continuously watching. I remember not liking it and was very uncomfortable about it. It was not like he was watching out for our safety. There was some other reason.

"I believe the sexual abuse I experienced had later effects that included a lack of trust -- not trusting anybody and continually picking bad relationships. I, myself, am a recovering alcoholic. A lot of times I remember drinking to dull the pain. I knew I was hurting, but I did not know why ... I would drink, and the hurt would go away. Because I did not trust anybody, it took a long time until I would seek therapy.

"I do not let my stepfather control the basic aspects of my life, but I do not think I could confront him. I am terrified of him. It is hard to comprehend a lot of times that this man is sick. He was certified in psychology. He knew better.

"I am not strong enough to deal with confrontation. I know the type of person he is. I am not ready for him to tell me I am a liar when I know that I am not ....

"My mother says today that I was an affectionate child. Many times I sought love and attention from other people -- strangers because I was not getting any love from my stepfather. I used to go around the neighborhood as a child and visit a perfect stranger's house and ask them if they wanted to play. They just saw this little girl. They took her in, had milk and cookies and played. There was nothing wrong ..."

Homemaker's Story Of Childhood Abuse

Background:

This survivor is a 37-year-old female who was molested from age five to age 12 by her stepfather. She has had some therapy and is currently recovering from alcohol and drug abuses, such as cocaine. She is divorced from a 14-year marriage and has two children. This survivor is a homemaker, but has held various occupations, including working in a drug treatment center, as a reservationist, cosmetic representative, co-owner of a business she operated and as a helper in a restaurant.

"Out of the dysfunctional part of my life, I have never really gained any confidence in myself to go do something. I have attempted things ...." she says. She reports of having attempted suicide five times and has confided the sexual abuse in various people, including her former husband, sisters, mother and therapists. She is currently involved in a relationship with a man she feels is very generous and kind. Her mother is now divorced from this survivor's stepfather.

Disclosing The Abuse

"I let it out at thirty when I was in the hospital. I told my sister then. My family could not understand why I was in the hospital. I started talking about my stepfather in an angry tone. I tore up his pictures in the middle of the hallway at the hospital.

"My sister turned around, and said, 'Do you think you are the only one it happened to?' It happened to both of my sisters. (One of my sisters is thirty-five years old now, and the other is thirty-three.) I learned that he had gotten one of my sisters pregnant, and she had an abortion, which none of the rest of us knew about.

"She was approximately seventeen or eighteen when it happened. My youngest sister will not talk about the abuse she experienced, but she does admit that it happened to her. She will not talk about it like my other sister and I do. She will not open up. Neither of my sisters have had therapy, although one of them has done a lot of reading on the subject. This particular sister goes overboard in protecting her children. When I brought this out, this sister told me that she had told her husband years ago. They had never mentioned it to the rest of

the family, but he helped her and stood by her and has worked with her. My husband did not, however.

"I got married in 1973, and our divorce became final in 1986. Before he left me I had been going to therapy for about two years. I was building my self-esteem and my pride. Then, there were things that were coming out of me that I thought I could never do or accomplish. It was like I was free again. It was like I had just let something out ....

Flashbacks Helped Her Remember

"I had started having flashbacks. During the flashbacks, I would see my stepfather over me when I was in bed with my husband. I was actually taking my hands and pushing my husband right off me and running to the bathroom. I did not know why. I felt then I could never tell him. It was a secret. When you live a secret all your life, you do nothing else but want to keep secrets. You feel there is nothing you can share with anyone.

"During the time I noticed something was wrong, one of my children was six. Something started bothering me. I was still seeing my stepfather then. He would come down on weekends and go fishing with my husband and spend the whole weekend with us .... All of a sudden, I started having short-term affairs. I mean one-nighters. These things just tore me up. I would feel so much remorse. Then, I would come home and tell my husband like I wanted to punish him. That's what came out in therapy. Actually, what I was wanting to do was punish my stepfather. 'Ha ha. I got you. You are not home enough. I am going to go out and have my fun' sort of thing ....

"I got married at nineteen. My husband was my everything to me ... We ended up having a beautiful home with an in-ground pool. We accomplished a lot. He went through college. We had our own business, cars, an airplane -- the whole nine yards. When I let everything out, he told me that he hated me and left me about a year after I told him. I found out later he had been having a relationship for about a year and a half before he even broke up with me, and I thought that things were getting better ...."

Suicide, Sex And Therapy

"I have tried to commit suicide five times. The most devastating time was the night my husband told me that he was leaving me. Once our business started, he was traveling a lot. It got to the point where all I did was spend money and shop. My husband would go off flying or playing golf.

"We sort of started separating. Our sex life was not good either...."I have gone through two years of sexual therapy. Before therapy, I did not realize that I was ashamed of my own body ....

"I hurt a lot when my husband left me. He told me he hated me for what I let out. My whole family was destroyed by our divorce. When he left, I sat in the kitchen one night and took all the pills I could find with alcohol. I ended up in intensive care for a couple days.

"My girlfriend stayed there with me. I managed to con the doctor into letting me go home. I told him that I was just fine. It was then I started realizing what was really happening to my life, my marriage. Through the years, I had let my father and husband get very close.

"My husband was a very quiet person. I never knew who I was involved with. People normally talk in a relationship. We never did. Now, I can look at what our entire marriage represented. It is not something that should have been a loving, caring relationship. I mean, he showed up at the hospital, and he sent me roses, but he did not support me emotionally. When I look back now, it was like I was the only one going through it. My husband was not involved in my recovery.

Confronting The Offender

"I confronted my stepfather before I got out of the hospital. I confronted him on the telephone. I could not go home without letting him know that I remembered what happened to me. I had written down what I wanted to say on paper. It was not that long. I told him that he was not going to have control over my life, my feelings and my emotions. He said, 'I have not had control over you in a long time.' He never admitted or denied what he did.

"My stepfather worked with newspapers for twenty-five years and then went into the restaurant business. My mother is a nurse. I did not find out that my stepfather was my stepfather until I was fifteen years old. When I found out, it was almost like a relief. It was like, 'Thank God you are not my father! Thank God you are not my father!' He (her stepfather) told me that he loved me as a father. I wanted to scream and yell. I wanted to beat him up because all my life I had to pretend ...

"When I first checked myself into a hospital ... This was the time I had told my sister about the sexual abuse. I thought I had gone to the hospital because of the affairs I had been having. Once I was there, I did not want to see my husband. So, he had the housekeeper bring all my clothes. He could not understand why I did not want to see him.

"My therapist started working with me. I remember one day sitting in my room ... I started throwing things around. I let it all out. I had been too scared to tell anyone. I was afraid to tell anyone in the hospital. I was afraid they were not going to like me. During this time, I tried to kill myself. I had asked the nurse to give me a razor to shave my legs. They gave me a safety razor ... I always could con. This was a dysfunctional way of getting my way ....

"In group therapy, another woman started talking about the sexual abuse she had gone through. I remember my therapist asked me if I had anything to say. I remember thinking that he tricked me, and then I had to bring it up. It was like freedom, but at the same time, I still thought, 'What was my husband going to think of me?' "

"I remember how he (stepfather) used to play with us. He would take blankets and make them like tents. He would get under the blankets with us and play tent. My mom would be sitting right in the next room. He would do things to me, touching and kissing. It was almost like it became a game. At this time, I was twelve years old. I was getting older ....

"I have spoken with doctors and learned that stimulation is a thing that you become used to. I had been stimulated by him for so many years. I did not know what it was. I did not know what stimulation was... I have read in books that the sexual need for a man is not there ... I constantly worry, 'Am I okay? Am I normal?' "

Dysfunctional Atmosphere Welcomes Offender

" .... My mother checked herself into hospitals a lot when I was growing up. She was being treated for alcoholism. I had a lot of household responsibilities then. I had to cook dinner and help around the house a lot when she was gone. This is when he would do things to me.

"There is one thing that sticks in my mind more than anything. I had to have been five or six years old. I remember him standing me on the toilet and putting his penis between my legs and rubbing me all over. He did not penetrate me. I can't remember anything else except that he would ejaculate all over me. I did not understand. I did not think anything ....

"I remember going home to mom and finding out that I was illegitimate. Now, my mother is beginning to talk with me about those years. I was talking to my mother the other day, and I asked her about her relationship with my stepfather when they were married. She told me she married my stepfather six months after I was born. She waited to divorce him until all the children were grown. She told me that her sexual relationship had been bad. In all the years of therapy that my mother went through, she never let it out that she suspected something was happening with her husband and daughters. I think she was afraid. That's why she kept going to hospitals. She was too scared to let it out.

"My stepfather was her security. Their marriage was her blanket. We lived in beautiful homes most of our lives. My stepfather had a good job, and we had the typical vacations of two and three a year. We did everything, but when you came into the house, everything was different ....

"My stepfather used to work nights .... I would sleep in bed with my mother. He would come home and carry me to bed. At that time, I was in the third grade. I failed the fifth grade. They (teachers) saw it. I was making nothing but Ds and Fs in the fifth grade. I remember getting into fights with children on the bus. I remember having a very bold teacher. She had red hair. She pushed me up against the bathroom wall and told me that I was going to listen to her.

"It was always like I was in fear. I did not even take up for myself. I did not tell my mother what happened. I think this teacher saw the symptoms of abuse, but she did not call my mom. In those years, no one knew how to deal with anything, but she was punishing me for something I had done on the bus. She did not realize how afraid I was ....

"I remember I used to sit at the table. I used to get smacked in the head by my parents because I was either reading too slow or not fast enough or not working productively enough for them. Why did any of this happen? " ....My sister called me last year and told me my uncle had committed suicide. He did not leave a note. Our aunt, his former wife, is now married to my stepfather.

"My cousin told my sister that her father -- my uncle, sexually abused other children and then said, 'Your father (stepfather) tried it with me.' She said that I intervened, but I don't remember it. These are the things that are so scary because I thought everything was already out. When am I going to remember this?

"I remember her coming to visit us when we were children. She told my sister over the phone that our father -- my stepfather came into the room and went over to her bed, and I got up and pulled him over to my bed or something. I don't remember it. She was crying ....

"After my stepfather's brother committed suicide, my cousin told my sister that she had been abused by both these men. My cousin is receiving therapy ... When we were growing up, my sisters and I just wanted to get away from the family. When I was in school, I could not concentrate. I do not know what it was, but I just could not think.

" ... I can look back on my life now and see how I lived so dysfunctionally because of the incest. The biggest thing now is that I have to deal with my fears. I have tremendous fears. If I have a *conflict with someone, I either get passive or aggressive, but not assertive. I have tried to work on assertiveness. But I get scared that me trying to get a point across is going to bring rejection ....*

"So many times in my life, I still feel like a little child. I feel like a six, seven, eight year old girl who is going outside to play or to have a tea party. I have to talk with myself to get myself straight."

What We Can Do To Prevent Opportunities For Offenders

We can prevent by understanding the opportune times offenders chose to offend. We can prevent the opportunities from arising by not allowing our children to be alone in the presence of family/individuals or others who have noted, suspected or confirmed psychological abnormalities or peculiarities, or drug or alcohol addictions. If suspected individuals often demonstrate antisocial behavior coupled with inappropriate immaturity in light of their ages, that might be cause for concern too.

Single mothers should take special care in who they date -- guarding against bringing anyone into the home who may have drug or alcohol problems. Single mothers, I believe, are the targets of some opportunistic offenders. Single mothers give opportune offenders seemingly easy access to children.

A common place for sexual assault of children occurs in their own beds! Offenders who look for opportunities to rape or play out other sexual fantasies, do so often by intruding upon the sleep of children. Beds are normally safe refuges for most children, but for the survivor, bed may be a symbol of unrest, tormenting memories of trying to remove and push away the offender's hands from private areas and the common offender's warning: *"Don't tell anybody!"*

If a family member sees or notices an extended family member or step-parent or neighbor-friend of the family entering and exiting a room that a baby or child may be sleeping in, and this person has little to do with caring for that baby or child, I would certainly question his or her presence and motivation for being in that room! I certainly would not allow such a person to be alone with a child or baby.

Teenagers can be instructed to read books that present and instill morals. Teaching and demonstrating respect for privacy, respect for others by being courteous to another's feelings and rights as a human being may be a start for some. Dysfunctional behavior of any sort often lays the ground for more of the same.

Teachers should make it a point to routinely familiarize themselves with physical and emotional signs of abuse, which are often open doors to potential sexual abuse. Teachers can use their roles as instructors to include the role of confidante. They should be concerned if students appear stressed and have poor grades or notable declines in grade performance or problems concentrating. (Read *Chapter IV: What Are The Signs Of Sexual Abuse?* for more information on emotional and physical signs.)

Preventing child sexual abuse may have countless steps because of the complexities leading up to it. People who are sexually abused by a brother or a sister or cousin are usually living within the confines of ticking time bombs -- the bombs being the offenders.

Some of the offenders in these cases were victimized sexually through another family member or by an outsider or through pornographic materials and/or endured emotional cruelties as children. The families in these situations may be surviving with all sorts of dysfunctions within the midst. Refer to this book's second *Prevention Checklist For Chapter II* in the back of this chapter for possible solutions on mapping out a personal prevention plan.

Realities

The abuser continues to carry and sow threads of destruction long after he or she has stopped pursuing his or her fantasies with a particular victim. The frightening thing is that the offender moves on to another victim. The offender does not recognize his or her infringement upon the unsuspecting child or the potential devastation for a victim's loved ones -- the ones who care for the child. (Some do, but this sort is discussed in Chapter III in detail.)

What an offender may know intellectually from sermons or laws or rules for good social behavior, he does not believe to be true because he puts his need to fulfill his desires and fantasies first. Most offenders believe their actions are harmless; however, they know not to express their true beliefs in front of anyone who might turn them into the authorities or attempt to stop them. They know enough about what society expects from citizens to fake true citizenship. (See *Chapter III: Sexual Offenders -- Who Are They?* for more information.)

The following interviews provide another facet of the legacy of destruction sexual offenders leave their victims to contend with. Survivors who were abused by their own brothers have tremendous guilt because they often hate their offenders and feel immobile in their attempts to protect themselves. They feel trapped with their own recognition of their offender's status within their family. They are afraid they will not be believed and if believed, they fear they will be abandoned or rejected and regarded as being unworthy of respect and love. Their feelings of guilt prompts them to question their own self-worth or value. They question whether they could have stopped the offender's intrusive actions.

Three Accounts From Women Survivors Sexually Abused By Their Brothers

"Do not have sexual relations with your sister, either your father's daughter or your mother's daughter, whether she was born in the same home or elsewhere." --- Leviticus 18:09. (NIV).

Environmentalist's Story Of Childhood Abuse

Background:

The following victim is a 29-year-old woman who was sexually abused by her older brother. She recalls two separate incidents. (She is unable to recall the exact age and speculates she may have been seven or eight years old when the second incident occurred and four years old during the first assault.) This survivor says she may have blocked much of the abuse out. She is a college graduate, divorced from a four-and-a-half year marriage. She works as an environmentalist. She has shared her experiences with close friends, her older sisters and former husband and had, at the time of the interview, six sessions of professional counseling.

Recollections

"I was four years old. One of my sisters and I were playing ... There were trees and woods, and I remember that we were standing close to a creek. My sister was crying. Now, I understand he was trying to make her go into the woods. She refused, so he told her he was going to take me. And that is when he led me into the woods. I knew he was upset. He carried me off, and I don't remember him talking that much. Basically, he raped me. He took my panties off. He forced himself inside me. I remember it hurt, and that I did not know what he was doing. I didn't understand sex, and then I do remember that he was twelve years old ....

"The incident that occurred when I was seven basically amounted to him forcing me into oral sex .... He was fifteen years old then ... I was real shy when I was little. I remember the following day after the rape in the woods, I had pain in my vaginal area. I felt very dirty.

"My mother knows my brother hurt me, but she does not really know what he actually did. She has never asked me any questions. I am very grateful because I have gone through so many discoveries. She has told me she has always felt something was wrong. I am sure she does not know any specifics. She asked me if he hurt me mentally or physically. I told her he had, but that is all ...

"My brother is the black sheep of the family. My parents knew he had problems growing up, and they tried to help him, but nothing worked. He does not say much, and when he does, I think he is aggressive.

"...He does not talk. He does not communicate, and at the same time, he has a heavy hand with his own children. He married when I was seventeen. His oldest son got married last year, and I have a grandniece. My brother has three boys. He works in construction. I think his marriage and work is moderately successful. He has been married for close to twenty years. During this time, I doubt he has ever had therapy.

Results Of Therapy

"... I feel like I am getting better since I started treatment for the sexual abuse. I have learned to love myself and admitted what my brother did was pretty cheap. I have realized it was not my fault. When I was twenty-three years old, I started realizing that what my brother did was wrong; however, I still have an insatiable desire to be accepted.

"I want to be accepted, but I feel that I am not, but I am not a clutcher. I want a loving relationship, but I am also shy about that.

"...There was a time when I did not have any self-esteem. I would go to bed with anybody who liked me halfway. To have sex with anybody was just a different way of acceptance. I am a little afraid of a loving relationship now. I think this may be due to having had relationships with the wrong men than having been sexually abused ...."

Associations: Memory Links To The Past

"When I was nine, my father and I were taking a nap together. He cuddled me. I had my back to him, and I got scared. It made me nervous. He was very affectionate and a good father. I know he was not trying anything. I associated it (the nap) somehow with what my brother had done. And I thought to myself, 'No I can't do this with him.'

"I think I might tell my mother sometime after my father dies. I know I can't tell my father ...."

Catch-22 Situation

"When I was six or five, I had a bad time with bedwetting. I remember feeling terrible because my mother would always get upset. A couple times, she would rub my face in it. What I am angry about is that she did not realize that it was a physical effect of something. When I was ten, I had another spat of bedwetting. A few months later, I started having severe pains on my left side. As it turned out, I had a cyst on my left kidney. It was bigger than a golfball. She said no wonder I was wetting the bed .... "

Dreams That Disrupt Sleep

".... I was suicidal when I was nineteen. Sometimes, I feel as though I don't really know how to mature. I dreamed once that a giant was chasing me. I was a little girl. It was a fairytale dream. I dreamed in black and white. I did not really associate it with the sexual abuse, but the dream was very real.

Disclosure

"I have talked with one of my sisters, some close friends and my former husband about the abuse. I was twenty-three years old before I told anybody. The incident that happened when I was four just recently came back to me in therapy. For the longest time, it did not occur to me that what had gone on was wrong.

".... I hated myself for about ten years. I felt that everything was wrong in the world. I looked for moral support and acceptance especially during those years. Rejection was a horrible thing. I eventually told both of my sisters, but even then I felt I had to be selective in who I told. I told the man I was married to, and he was semi-supportive. He had the attitude that said: 'Gee, I am sorry that happened to you. I don't know what else to do for you.' He knew it was a bad thing, and I guess he wondered why I had not talked about it before. I later realized I was married to the wrong man for the wrong reasons.

"After talking with my sisters, I discovered my brother had tried to do things to them. For me, to talk was a relief. I learned two of the girlfriends I told had also been abused. I told three men friends. Two of them were very supportive. One was confused. He did not know why I was sharing this with him. He said, 'I feel embarrassed that this happened to you. But, I don't know how I can help you.' I feel that I have to be able to let go of the past, the pain. Carrying that around serves no purpose .... "

Confronting The Perpetrator

"I wrote my brother a couple letters. I didn't really say anything. Just, 'You know what you did, and I need you to ask me for my forgiveness. He didn't respond. But, I did forgive him. Then, I felt like the weight had been lifted from my shoulders. I think what he did was wrong. He should not have done it. I do not feel I will ever love him like I once did, as a brother. When I was younger, I did love him very much.

"After the second incident, he cut all contact with the family off ... When he came back into contact with the family, he did not talk to me. I felt rejected. I didn't connect it. I think this is why I had such a hard time dealing with rejection. Anytime I talk about it now, I have *this fear.*

"During therapy, I started piecing things together: being rejected by my brother and experiencing a form of rejection by a lover ... Under hypnosis, my therapist took me back in time. I got angry again because I was just about to forgive my brother for the incident that occurred when I was seven or eight, but then I discovered something else, the rape at the age of four."

Nurse's Story Of Childhood Abuse

Background:

The following account is from a 39-year-old female who was sexually abused from age seven to age nine by her brother who is four years older. The victim is currently a nurse. She has had some therapy and is presently participating in group therapy for adult women who were sexually abused as children. She has confided in one of her siblings. She has also attempted suicide.

Recollections

"I blocked out the incidents for several years until 1982. I started having nightmares. In the dream, my brother was the giant, and I was the little girl.

" ... (In reality) He (her brother) fondled and touched me a lot for a long time when I was a child. I dream about him now. I dream about him doing it. I wake up terrified, and I cry. When I wake up, it is like I am still a little girl. I cry for a while, and then I seem to get better ....

"I told my younger sister about the dreams and the abuse when I was thirty-two. She was twenty-six years old then. She knew something was wrong. I told her that our brother had sexually abused me as a child ... I begged her not to tell anybody. Of course, I was able to tell her more details about the abuse later.

"Although telling my sister helped, I did begin drinking real heavy. I attempted suicide, so I began seeing a therapist. It was through therapy that I realized how the effects of the abuse were affecting other areas of my life. I have two doctors now ...

Confronting The Offender

"When I was in the hospital, I wrote my brother a letter, but he didn't respond. I told him that I felt what he had done was not fair. I told him he was supposed to protect me. When I got the courage to tell my father, I told him that my brother had ruined my life because of the abuse. Although my father does not give me any emotional support at all, he is helping me pay the hospital bills. Nobody understands in my family. My mother died two years ago. I would have never considered telling her when she was alive.

"My brother is very mean and vindictive. I do not know why he wants to pick on me and my little sister. He wrote my mother a letter before she died telling her terrible lies about me and how I should stand on my own feet and take care of my own bills. This made me feel crummy. His letter reinforced the bad feelings I have about myself. I have a terrible self-image. Sometimes, I feel that I am not worth anything. I do not let my friends -- especially men, get too close. My brother has had power over me all these years. I am trying not to let that continue.

"... In the letter I wrote him (her brother), I said he ruined my life and that he should take responsibility for what he did. My therapist helped me write the letter. It was more of a letter of how I felt. I still have a lot of anger. I have only seen my brother twice since 1982. Both times were due to deaths in the family, funerals."

".... My family did not know anything about this until I went into the hospital ... I had a lot of problems with depression. I did not tell my dad about the abuse until I was hospitalized a second time. I felt like I had to deal with it in my own way. Daddy doesn't know what to do. This is just how he is. He just wants me to forget about it."

Feelings Towards Brother Now

"I think if I saw him now, I would beat him to a bloody pulp."

Recollections Of Childhood Abuse From University Student

Background:

The following account is from a 21-year-old female university student. She was sexually abused from age 11 to age 14 by her brother who is six years older and has Klinefelter syndrome. (Klinefelter syndrome is a chromosome abnormality, where the male usually has two X chromosomes and one Y chromosome. The presence of an extra X chromosome may result in no sperm formation, small testicles and sterility.)

She has undergone eight weeks of professional therapy and is, at the time of this interview, in line for additional therapy through a county department. She says she has run up thousands of dollars in medical bills due to health problems and exploratory surgeries. Her health problems include nervous system disorders, panic attacks and heart problems, which require beta blockers. She also suffers from bouts of severe anger and depression. This young woman has dropped in and out of college, but presently has started again.

Recollections

"*The first time we were outside. This is the first time I remember. It could have happened before, but this is the first time I remember. We were at my grandmother's. We were playing in the yard. I don't remember how we got there, but we ended up in the bushes. That was the first time it happened. I tried to push him off, but he is (was) six foot two.. He is taller than that now. At the time, he was at least a couple hundred pounds. There was not much I could do. I asked him to stop it ... That is the first time I can remember. It*

86

could have happened before, and I just don't remember.

"I have specific memories of certain times ... Most the time, it would be that I would be asleep in my bedroom with my sister. He would come in, and he would start doing something ... just fondling me ... and then I would wake up. At first, I tried to push him off. I was too scared to scream, and I really didn't want anyone to know. I would try and push him off, but again he was so big. I was too scared to yell or scream. I was ashamed of what happened to me ... I would usually wake up with him on top of me ... Eventually, he started forcing me to have intercourse with him. I remember asking him to stop ... After a while, I began to think that it was my fault. At times, I still do.

Disclosure

"The first time I told someone was in the summer of 1987. I was seventeen years old and was going through orientation at college. I was rooming with my best friend from high school. I told her. At first, she was very supportive. Then, as time went on through our freshman year, I started having problems. I guess because I thought my whole life had been focused on getting away from home and getting away from my brother. I had finally gotten into college. I thought all my problems would disappear, and when they did not, I started having emotional problems. I started doing bad in school. I did not have any motivation to work.

"My roommate got really tired of me and the problems that were surfacing. She told me that when I was in the room I would be very upset. I would be crying, and she would bring people into the room ... and she would tell me that she did not give a damn about my problems. She said she did not want me to be upset in the room because she did not want to have to live through it.

"...Her father was a doctor. She thought no one had problems as bad as her father's. She totally abandoned me. That is when I started seeing a psychologist at school ....

"Basically, my roommate was the only person who knew about the abuse for seven months. I had thought that if I had a problem, I could keep confiding in her. I did not want a lot of people knowing. I remember coming home one day, and her telling me that her mother thought I should go to church for help. And I said, 'Wait a minute. What do you mean? Your mother?'

"She told me that she had talked about my problems with her mother. I threw an absolute fit. We got into a fight. Everyone on the floor heard it, yelling, screaming and cussing. Then, she went out somewhere, and I happened to notice a letter from her sister.

"Come to find out, her mother knew, her father knew, her sisters and brothers knew. This made me very upset. When she came back, our argument continued. She said: 'If you are as unhappy as you seem to be, and you hate living as much as you do, why don't you just kill yourself because everyone would be better off.' This argument ended everything. She had totally betrayed me."

Past And Present Fears

" .... My brother has no idea what effect this has had on me. He came up to me once and said, 'Whatever I did to make you hate me so much, I am sorry.' But, he has never admitted or acknowledged what he did. When I think about what he did to me, I sometimes get confused, depressed. I hate the fact that I have so much anger. It scares me. When I go back home, I drive there and come back to school all in the same day. I just hope that if I have to go to my house or something that he won't be there. When I am there and if he comes in, I basically sit there and do not acknowledge him. He talks to me, and I do not answer him. I avoid him. I do not want anything to do with him.

".... I had to spend a night at my parents house when my grandmother died. His presence made me feel he was trying to rob me of saying goodbye to my grandmother ... I remember when my brother was diagnosed with Klinefelter syndrome. He was causing a lot of problems at the house. He had a lot of hate built up inside him because he blamed my parents. My father drank a lot then, but I don't recall him being an alcoholic.
"I remember his (her brother's) fights and him walking out of the house after tearing up the Christmas tree.... "He would, on occasions, hit me, but my father never did. My brother put his fists through the walls and slammed doors. He tore up everything we owned. He would get into a fight with my parents and put his fists right through the wall.

"I remember when my brother would push me and hold me down. There is no way an eleven year old girl could fight that much pressure ... Since then, he has been in and out of jail .... "I know that he attempted something with my sister. I think he tried to kiss or fondle her. For some reason, it did not go that far. I know that she *has not forgotten about it. I think she has forgiven him.*

"I know that he tried something with my sister's child. I know because my sister asked me what would happen if she took her daughter to the doctor and had her examined, and the doctor found she had been abused. I told her that the doctor would have to report the abuse to the authorities, the police and social services.

"When I told her that she said, 'Well, I am not going to do it. I do not want to get him into any trouble.' My niece is about four years old. I do not think my sister could handle the scandal of everything coming out. My mother knows. My sister knows.

"...My dad asked my mother why I did not want to come home during breaks or weekends. He does not know anything about it. He kept pressing my mom for a reason as to why I won't come home. She told my dad that my brother had tried something, but there is no way that she would tell him that my brother sexually abused and raped me.

"I have absolutely no meaningful thoughts of my father. I am not close to him. The only thing my father and I talk about are sports. I find it very difficult to express anything to my parents. Yet, I have gotten to the point where I can say anything to my mom because I basically don't give a damn what she thinks of me. I have gotten over worrying that she does not love me as much as she loves my sister or that she resents me because of what happened. She knows what happened, and she has to deal with it ...."

Notes On Prevention

Preventing older siblings from sexually abusing younger siblings boils down to preventing abuse and domestic violence period. Some child offenders have been sexually abused themselves and *'act out'* on other children. Some have been additionally exposed to pornographic materials and other forms of violence and abuse. Prevention of sexual abuse partially means education -- an awareness of what sexual deviancy is. It means to arm ourselves and children with information. It means to foster communication about protection against intruders or offenders.

Making it a point to develop and use open discussions on the importance of protecting oneself from any sort of abuse will increase the likelihood of a child fighting back, running away from the offender and telling a trustworthy adult. Determining who a trustworthy adult is can be difficult for children to discern. It is imperative that they be told that they are entitled to call the police, sheriff and/or social service departments and inform authorities of any abuse they have experienced. They should be told that they will not get into trouble by telling the truth or reporting even threats of sexual abuse.

Children should be told that they have the right to protection, that their bodies belong to themselves. It is not necessary to try and explain the motivations of a sexual deviant to children in order to protect them. It is not necessary to even mention the word: "*sex.*"

Children should be told that sometimes people who appear good may do bad things and that sometimes people we love do bad things. Children can and should be taught the importance of self-protection through age-appropriate books on subjects that promote good self-esteem. A book titled: *LOVING TOUCHES, A BOOK FOR CHILDREN ABOUT POSITIVE, CARING KINDS OF TOUCHING* by Lory Freeman (for grades preschool and up) emphasizes to children as young as two years what normal behavior is.

Another book for children that parents can use as a prevention tool in teaching young children is titled: *MY BODY IS PRIVATE* by Linda Walvoord Girard (for grades K-3). You might also scan your local book stores and libraries for appropriate children's books.

Parents, teachers and anyone who cares for children should make it a point to keep the lines of communication open, respectful, non-threatening. Initiating conversation and having a verbal rapport may reveal clues of abuse having occurred or the threat of abuse. Open communication may prevent situations from evolving into sexual abuse when children feel safe in divulging threatening situations to caretakers or parents.

While some victims of sexual abuse are approached in their own beds or homes by baby-sitters or relatives or friends of the family or neighbors, some victims are approached and even abducted from their homes by strangers. This is why it is so important that children be taught as soon as they are able to comprehend danger, how to lock and unlock doors and windows, use keys and house alarms or even fire alarms in buildings if they are being pursued by someone and need to draw attention. They should be taught how to hide if necessary if the danger of an intruder presents itself to them. They should also be taught how to confirm the identities of police officers by calling 911 before opening any doors to anyone claiming to be one.

Personal alarms and self-defense classes may give added assurance to some. Children should be prepared to anticipate very loud noise from alarms in the event they need to use one. Children might become distracted with additional fear when they hear an alarm for the first time. They should be told that in the event they use it, to pull the pin out and run as fast as they can to safety.

Although defense classes may or may not help a child physically fight off an adult, they can help children in other ways. Self-defense classes may supply other information about personal protection and foster feelings of being worthy of protection, of being important, thus, increase self-esteem. Offenders are not as likely to target children who give any indication that they may suddenly shout or run or cause a scene. They target children who appear vulnerable to assault. It is also quite possible that the visual presence of a personal alarm might deter an offender from approaching a child.

Man's Recollections Of Child Sexual Abuse By A Teacher

Background:

The following account is from a 51-year-old businessman. He was molested at age 11 by one of his teachers. He says the molestation was "*an isolated incident,*" yet he believes it had some influence on him experiencing intense shyness and problems communicating with others as an adult. The man suffered from gynecomastia, the overdevelopment of males' breasts in otherwise normal males, until it was surgically corrected at the age of 22.

This survivor says that an attempted molestation occurred at the age of 12 when three boys, ages 12 and 14, attacked him and touched his bottom over the top of his pants and attempted to pull his pants off. This victim has had a year of therapy and approximately five years of what he refers to as "*dianetics.*"

He explains that "*dianetic*" therapy has allowed him a release of tensions, frustrations and intense shyness in his adult life and a sort of desensitization from bad childhood experiences. He is divorced and has been married twice. He has children from his former marriages.

Recollections

"I was molested in school. The teacher -- a man, grabbed me in the chest. I never told anyone. I believe that the incident has changed my personality. I never told my parents. For me, it was a terrible experience ....

"My class went to the beach as a field trip. I swam to the deep part of the ocean. My feet did not touch the bottom. My teacher said, 'Come to me. I will help you. I will hold you.' He swam to the deeper part of the water and took a hold of me. He turned me around and started rubbing my chest in a sexual way. When I realized that he was being sexual with me, I swam away from him.

"... I saw my teacher about four years ago. He was standing on a corner waiting for a bus. He did not see me. He looked so old. If I could confront my teacher now about what he did to me, I would tell him 'I am the student you molested, and that because of the molestation, I have suffered. If he were twenty years younger, I would tell him, and I would make charges against him ....

"Some boys I thought were my friends tried to take my pants down and have sex with me ... They tried to hold me down. They touched my behind over my pants and threw me on the floor. I fought back. I hit them, and they ran away from me. I went to the house where the two twelve-year-olds lived. I told their aunt, and she said they would be punished for what they had done to me.

"I felt betrayed and humiliated for what they had tried to do to me. I thought we had been close friends. When I was a boy, I planned my revenge. I told myself that when I was bigger I was going to get them back. I was trying to prove that I was a male because I had breasts *like a female. I wanted them to know that I am a male ....*

"Because of these things, I became aggressive. I wanted respect and tried to get it by being aggressive ... I remember throwing a big chair to the floor when I was a teenager ..."

Account From A Woman Sexually Abused As A Child By Her Natural Father And Her Father's Friends

Teacher's Story Of Childhood With Ongoing Emotional, Physical and Sexual Abuse

Background:

The following account is from a 40-year-old woman who was abused not only sexually by her natural father, but emotionally and physically as well. Her victimization began when she was a few days old. The sexual abuse continued until age 13, but the other abuses continued well into her teen life. The abuses did not stop with her father.

She was sexually abused by a dentist, a busdriver and some of her father's male friends. She was subjected to severe emotional cruelties from her aunts throughout her childhood. Although well-recuperated now, this adult survivor labels herself as having been the "scapegoat" of her family.

Her grandparents on both sides of the family had knowledge of the emotional and physical abuses -- but did not raise any seemingly caring concerns for her physical and emotional well-being. This survivor found help through a church and the

96

love of a sister-in-law who led her to it. There, she found true understanding, forgiveness and a total cleansing and healing of spirit.

Until this time, she had undergone extensive therapy and counseling. She had been labeled by psychiatrists and therapists as being schizophrenic, a manic depressive, being atypical psychotic and having multiple personality disorder (now known as Dissociative Identity Disorder [DID]).

This survivor says she also suffered from severe delusions and hallucinations. She had a history of suicidal thoughts and attempts, including throwing herself down a flight of stairs at the age of four -- having been convinced by her abusers and their actions that she was *bad and unworthy of love.* Presently, she is a successful teacher, having received awards for her professional skills. She is a college graduate and married with one child. She calls her account, *"the classic horror story."*

Recollections

"My father was an alcoholic. To give you an idea about the severity in which we lived, my father tried to kill me when I was only a few days old by throwing me out a window. From there, it continued.

"My mother was a very passive woman. My mother and father had gotten married because my mother had gotten pregnant with me. My father was about twenty-eight years old then. I believe that was really the source of my father's anger toward me. I also think that he was jealous that there was someone else getting my mother's attention. I have a younger sister who was also abused. She was not sexually abused like I was; however, she was battered ....

"It seemed that after a while I kind of took the place of my mother. I became a parent to my mother, my sister and even my father. My father had knowledge that a busdriver had abused me, but he did not know about the dentist abusing me. My father would arrange for his friends to come over to the house. They would all be drunk. They would molest me. My earliest recollection of the physical abuse goes back as far as I can remember ... from birth on.

"The sexual abuse started around age four and ended about age thirteen. My father's physical abuse became almost murderous. I think he saw his sexual abuse toward me as almost like affection ....

"My father had so much rage in him directed at me. So many things in his life were falling apart .... It was real hard for him to deal with me in a mature manner. He had a difficult time dealing with me developing into a teenager and an adult. My mother did nothing to protect me from my father when I was growing up; however, she did on occasion when he was getting rough say, 'Now, _____ , that's enough.' But, she did not say it too loudly because he went after her too. At times, it was just as bad for her as it was for me.

"... My father died after open heart surgery some time ago. I never confronted him about what he had done to me. In my family, we had to pretend. We had the outside world and then, our home, which was hell. I thought everybody lived that way. We always kept up the pretense. I did not discover that other people did not live that way for a long, long time ....

"There were times when my abuse became apparent to people outside my family. I described very innocently one day in kindergarten one of the things my father had done to me. The teacher and class were talking about families and parents. I don't remember exactly what I said, but I had said something about my father hurting me. I did not think anything about saying what I did was unusual.

"My grandparents knew about some of the abuse, but because they never did anything about it, I thought it was normal. My teacher asked me if I was telling the truth. She said, 'I think I need to talk with you alone, and later I agreed she could talk with my mother. I realized that this was something I could get into trouble for. The teacher came to my house and spoke with my mother who basically told her I was lying. My mother made it clear to me that I was not to tell anyone else about what was happening to me after this ...

"Another time, I was in the hospital for a related injury, and I was covered in scars and other injuries from the abuse. The nurse said, 'Who did this to you? right in front of my mother. By this time, I was around eight. I looked at my mother, and I did not say anything. It was a clear message that I was not to share this with anybody ....

"I had my first gynecological exam when I was thirteen years old. I did not know anything about the facts of life or any of the proper terms for anything. My mother was with me. The doctor asked her if she had spoken with me about any of these things. She had not because in our house that was such a taboo subject.

"There was never anyone I could confide in. I had the feeling of complete helplessness. Those people who abused me just covered it up, and the people you might expect to help me, turned their backs on the situation. That -- for me, was really a major issue -- the sense of having no control ....

"My father was very disturbed. At one point, my father directly told me that he could no longer beat and hurt me in the same ways he had in the past, but he said, 'I am going to destroy you psychologically.' He said, 'This is psychological warfare, and I am going to destroy you.'

"We had the kind of relationship where I was the enemy, and I was something to be destroyed. My mother is still living. We have talked about what he did to me. My healing has been complete, but for her it is still difficult. We talk about the troubles we went through with him, the scars and problems that developed because of them and the spiritual healing I have received since. I forgive her completely. I do not have an axe to grind with her. She is close to sixty now ....

"My father was fifty-two years old when he died. I did not cry at first. My husband and I received a telegram saying that my father had died. My father had been in the hospital. Drinking and smoking like he did, destroyed his heart. He lived life in tenth gear. He was an emotional wreck. My response to my father's death is a real indicator of the ambivalence I had. I wanted him to love me. But, it was clear that he hated me. I was always trying to buy his love by doing well in school or trying to please him in other ways...

"When my husband told me my father died, I smiled. I wanted to laugh. I was so happy. I just hated him that much. Then, I felt real guilty. I don't remember much more than that. It did not matter if he was dead or alive. The torment he left me with is still in me. Two days after we received the telegram, I called his third wife, a woman he married after my mother divorced him. I offered my condolences. My mother was his second wife. I know he abused his first wife, and that's why she divorced him.

"I got a letter from my father two days after he died. It was like he was reaching out of his grave. He paid me to write him ... He knew I would have no contact with him. When I was about seventeen, he had just about knocked me out. He smashed a lot of furniture and beat me up. It was a violent time. He tortured our dog with cigarettes and had been more violent than usual. That evening, I do not know how it got to that point, but he said he was sorry. He was crying. This is the only time I remember him apologizing. We all just stood there. We were all crying. The only other time I heard him express any kind of remorse was when I overheard him apologizing to my mother.

"My father was an unusual person. He had a photographic memory. He was very intelligent and good in science and math. He had incredible skills. He could pretty much do anything that he wanted. He used that skill in bizarre ways. He set up our entire house with wire and bugs, so that he could hear anybody talking in other rooms. He would shoot microphones at neighbors houses and became real paranoid about police....

"He had our house wired so that at every point he could hear police radio transmissions. Everytime I left the house, he would ask what street I was going down ... With other people he appeared to be congenial and polite. He belonged to many social organizations and had even started some. He was very well liked, but he was difficult to work with for those who knew him. He was extremely demanding. He eventually ended up in jobs where he designed pollution control systems. In this, he did not have to work closely with anyone. It was all his own work. He later designed electronic systems for production. He was a very capable person ....

"Although he functioned quite well in his work, he had other problems. He had homosexual relationships. I knew this because I picked him up from hotels, where he had been with men and prostitutes. He had gotten caught driving and drinking and lost his license. I became his wheels. Sometimes, we had to track him down. I would find him in a motel with a man. That was toward the end. It was a conflict within me for a long time....

"He was in the Air Force at one time. He was with a lot of women -- prostitutes and men -- especially when we were overseas. He did not go to college. This was something that was hard for him to handle. He was kicked out of high school for threatening to throw a teacher out of a window. He told me this.

"His only recollection of his father was being chased around the yard with an axe. His mother is an evil person. We believe that she murdered her younger sister. This sounds very bizarre, and that it could not be true, but it is. Some of his family used to go around and collect money for some church cause and then keep the money for themselves. When he was younger, he talked about these things ....

"He came from a large family. When he was a boy, he lived in a Pennsylvania town that had a glass factory. He lived in a rather old house with a coal chute where coal was dropped in from the outside. My father had done something that made my grandmother angry, so she put him in the coal chute in total dark and cold for three days. There were rats down there. She would ask him everyday if he was going to apologize, and he would refuse. She finally had to let him out. My father's people were very disturbed people ....

"I had aunts who were always coming out of mental institutions. We stayed with them after they came out. Part of the problems I had with one of my aunts, I still don't remember. I can refer to traumatic events -- not really knowing all the things that happened to me. I just remember parts of it.

"One of my aunts had a lot of electric shock treatments. She was kind of like a workhorse in the house. She was always trying to lure me down into the basement with her. She would trap me down there. My mother would insist that I go down there. My aunt would say, 'Now, don't tell anybody.' I don't really remember what she did. I just remember being real scared and her pushing me into the wall and holding me there. All of my father's siblings had been abused and tortured in various ways by their mother ....

"My parents were always trying to kill each other with poison. When I was seventeen, I became the food taster. I had to taste all the food before we ate. My father worked for a chemical company. He would bring home all these poisons. My mother had many strange illnesses, where she would be violently ill and doctors could not find anything. He had clearly poisoned her. She would try to get him back. She would poison the tea, so I started cooking. They both felt better about it ... I was real disturbed. There was no doubt about it. I was crazy. From the very beginning, I think it is quite apparent that a lot of it is genetic. My mother's family was not abusive toward me at all, but they did not do anything to help me. I grew up disturbed ....

"I think I was affected sexually by all the abuses I went through. In my adult life, I did not form close relationships with anybody. I did not trust anybody. When I was growing up, I could not have anyone over. My mother did not want me going over to anyone else's house. She would let my sister go, but she wanted me to stay at home. I was the one who held things together ....

"Even as a child, I had a lot of dissociations. I remember I woke up one day, and I was in a school. I did not know what school it was or where I was or how I got there. I was just walking in the school, and I did not know anyone around me. I suffered from hallucinations -- auditory and visual. I heard people telling me things ....

"During my adult life, I experienced the worst things in 1987. I tried to kill myself. I slashed my wrists and took an overdose of medication. This was not the only time I had tried to commit suicide.

"When I was four years old, I threw myself down a flight of stairs because I wanted to go to heaven. I was walking around with so much internal agony. If you could have seen it, it was like walking around with blood dripping out of my shoes. Despite the abuses and the after effects, I was very confident before 1987 in my work and that I would get better. I was a good teacher....

"I had a good relationship with my husband, a new baby and a brand new house ... I had started writing a book and finished it in July 1988. It was a fictionalized account of what happened to me. I made my husband read it. This was something that I had never been able to share. This was the safest way for me to share it with him.

" My husband got me into therapy when I first met him at age nineteen. From then on, I was in therapy a lot. I was suffering from a variety of symptoms, including multiple personality disorder ... I understood what had happened to me and what I needed to do. I had a lot of delusional symptoms....

"I believed that my father was going to come back after me and that he was following me everywhere. I saw him everywhere I went. I believed his bones were coming up in the trees, and the trees had knives, and that I was going to be slaughtered.

"My life internally was painful. I was doing an excellent job at work and taking care of my child, but all along I was abusing alcohol and tranquilizers. In 1988, my therapist referred me to a psychiatrist who wrote me prescriptions. It seemed that I could not get numb. Sometimes, I would be suffering from taking too much of the medications ....

"After the abuses, I sometimes panicked. I never knew when it would happen. I saw God as my father. I believed that Jesus had existed, but he was dead because my father killed him. I had a lot of delusions. It was like a battlefield. As much as I wanted to be a whole person, to be at peace, free and unburdened of these memories, I did not seem to be getting better.

"I exhausted every human avenue in my life to seek help. It seemed that there was nothing more I could do. I decided I was going to kill myself in 1988, and that I could not go back to the school where I taught. I no longer had any strength to put up a pretense ...."

Finding Answers to Heal -- Not Fester

"My sister-in-law told me I needed deliverance. I translated this into exorcism. I just had this image of myself that I was going to be filled with demons ...

and that there would be no more me. She started calling and telling me I should come to her church. One day when my husband was out of town, I had this incredible fear that he was going to die. He traveled around a lot. I felt he was in real danger. Every time he left, I really needed him here. My sister-in-law called and asked for him. I asked her why she called, and she said she sensed she needed to pray for her brother's safety. This is when I confided some of my problems in her. I shared a few things with her about my life. After that, she kept calling me....

"One time she read something from the Bible. (I had been to church when I was young. I could hardly make myself go. I felt so wicked and condemned. The church I went to then was dead. I had taught Sunday School. It was just a charade.) At this time, I was losing my ability to function. It took every bit of willpower and self-control I had....

"There were times I would just go home and drink and go to bed. I had tried to kill myself in June 1988 by taking an overdose of drugs, and then in July, I had an anaphylactic reaction to phenobarbital. I had gotten to the point where I decided I had nothing left to give my child or husband. We had arranged to take a trip out of town to visit his sister and the church she had mentioned on the telephone. I planned to commit suicide when we returned.

"I had planned my suicide at other times, but this time I could no longer function. I was empty. I told myself that I did not want any more treatment and that there was not any help for me. I had all these good therapists looking out for me and trying to help me get better. I had tried everything. I thought then that the whole idea about going to church was strange and that the people there might hurt me..."

"I thought I was going to die ....

"When I got there, instead of being afraid, I felt comforted. My sister-in-law was glowing, and she was smiling. I felt at peace all of a sudden. Everything that had been tormenting me just died ... My own child at the time was carrying scars in himself from my unpredictability. As I entered the church, I just had this sense of love.

"I realized then that I had never felt love. My sister-in-law had told me that the church praised God with songs, prayer and by raising their hands a lot. I thought the songs were really nice. I don't remember exactly what the minister said during his sermon, but I remember thinking he was speaking directly to me. All I basically got out of the sermon was, 'If you want this love, reach out and get it.' Then, I could not understand what he said, but I noticed all these people going to the front of the church. I did not understand what was going on, so I put my hand down. I later went to the front of the church. I did not know the Gospel. I had not read the Bible ... I knew bits and pieces of the Bible ... Even teaching Sunday School, I had not read the Bible. I had no idea what was going on, but I felt loved and different. For the first time in my life, I really felt love.

"At that time, I did not understand all that Jesus had to offer me. My sister-in-law told me that I still had an area in me that needed counseling and healing. She suggested that I talk with her minister during my visit. After attending church, it just seemed that things would come to mind from my past, and I would be healed as soon as they came. It was not like before when the memories came in the form of a flashback. In times before, I would instantly be there. I would be paralyzed. I would panic and be in a state of flight.

Now, memories of the abuses were coming to mind, and then they would just move away and go ....

"By the middle of the week, my sister-in-law and husband both felt I needed some counseling at the church. I said I was not sure. I was afraid. I did not know exactly what was going to go on. But, I did not feel tormented like I had ... I remember taking a shower and washing my hair. I heard a voice speak to me. It was very loud, but not angry. It was so powerful. It said, '_____ , do My will.' I kept washing my hair. It was so loud. I do not know if I heard it from the inside of my head or the outside. It was so clear. I do not know if anyone had been in there with me would have heard it or not. I had suffered from hallucinations. This was not the same. This was not a crazy thing. I knew right away that I needed to get some counseling. Again, the voice spoke. It said, '_____ , do My will.' ... This all happened during one week ....

"After church one day, my husband and I went upstairs to talk with the minister. We sat down. Then, a couple walked in. An older woman walked in. She had her hair piled high on her head like a beehive. She was wearing a canary yellow suit and a rhinestone pin that said: 'JESUS.' Her husband, who looked like he could be her son, introduced her. He was wearing this too tight polyester suit. I inquired as to what they were doing there and was told they were going to pray for me. Then, the minister came into the room. He did not know anything about me. All he knew is that my husband and I wanted to talk with him.

"He asked me why I was there, and I sort of summarized the troubles

I had experienced as a child and an adult ... I prayed out loud and forgave the people who had offended me. The minister prayed with me and through Jesus's name. I was healed. I was later baptized in the Holy Spirit. As soon as we finished praying, I could think more clearly. It was just incredible. I ran into the bathroom and saw myself for the first time in the mirror. Every other time I had looked at myself in the mirror, I had seen all kinds of things, tormenting delusions and visual distortions. It was so wonderful to see myself ....

"When I accepted Jesus as my Saviour, his blood washed everything that had happened to me away, clean ... It is easy to stand in judgment of God and say, 'Well, how could you allow this to happen?'

"I am beginning to see that there are a lot of purposes. We cannot dictate to God like He is a vending machine for healing. He allows trials of purchase, so that we will learn that through all those things He is with us. Nothing will separate us from His love ... He would not be able to give me the faith I have now had I not been through trial to see Him standing right there."

Prevention Summary And Checklist For Chapter II

The amount of effort victims use to survive emotionally makes it difficult for caretakers, teachers, parents or the people who love and care for them to detect that any wrongdoing has even occurred. We are able to recognize that sexually abused children may show drops in grade performance at school or a lack of interest in their studies. These things, however, are not always indicative of sexual abuse. We know many things about the physical and emotional signs to look for in *suspected* or *confirmed* cases. (See *Chapter IV: What Are The Signs Of Sexual Abuse?*) Preventing such atrocities from ever coming into existence is part of learning from the cases we do know about -- not just recognizing signs of possible victimization to prevent further abuse. By stopping one sort of abuse, we prevent others from occurring.

Sexual abuse is most always a hidden problem, and it is sometimes hidden by the very people who are supposed to be protecting our children. Victims are scapegoated in some families or by people who know them or by strangers who read about sexual abuse cases. Scapegoating does not get us further ahead in terms of prevention. It slows us down. It muddies the waters. It hides our resolutions.

Victims attempt to hide the abuse out of fears, shame and other roadblocks the offender manipulates as barricades to being found out. There are the mothers who want to step forward with knowledge of someone sexually offending their child or children; however, some of these mothers are afraid for themselves and the possible damaged reputations and humiliation that could come about publicly for them, the victims and their families.

When and if they muster the courage to do so, their child is or children are removed from her home, and the devastation is compounded. Truth about the long-term effects of child sexual abuse should be taken as words of warning and wisdom. I hope the accounts in this chapter provide a significant measure of relief in that victims know they are not alone and help can be found in the right places.

While one survivor indirectly labels the "*worst part*" as not being able to communicate to her parents or others that not one, but two adult figures in her life sexually violated her, other survivors, say the "*worst part*" is the ambivalence they feel toward the perpetrator and themselves. For others, the worst part is that the memories of having been sexually abused -- betrayed by people they trusted, are never far from their thoughts.

For some survivors I spoke with during the interview process, the "*worst part*" can not be verbalized. For society, the worst part is that we have failed to learn from history, and it repeats itself in many dysfunctions that we label too taboo to talk about or as stories only valuable enough for sensational entertainment or gossip.

Love is said to be the greatest gift of all. Prevention is love, and love is showing responsibility in the places that hold significant influence over the masses: families, churches and schools.

Prevention Checklist

__ Prevent opportunities offenders use by taking measures to insure your child is in the care of a responsible adult -- no former or current drug addicts, alcoholics or those who have demonstrated or diagnosed mental disease or those with any sort of criminal background.

__ If you are a drug addict or alcoholic obtain help and guidance from counselors and doctors. Do not abuse drugs and alcohol at least while caring for your children. Put your children into the care of responsible adults until you are able to resolve your addictions.

__ Open or leave open the doors of communication between you and your child or children or children entrusted to your care and instruction.

__ Encourage respect for one another among siblings.

__ Model respectful behavior.

__ Censor dysfunctional influences from your home. Some examples of this can be found in violent television programs or movies that contain violence and sex or violent sexual and language content. Other dysfunctional influences can come from violent and adult cartoons, pornographic magazines and books. More examples of dysfunctional influences are known or suspected sexual offenders, drug abusers, alcoholics or people who demonstrate regular violent behavior.

__ Obtain psychological advice and/or counseling for any child who demonstrates sexually deviant behaviors or physical violence. Obtain psychological advice and/or counseling if you feel emotionally out of control.

___ Discuss and explore possible prevention strategies with your children's teachers or the school board of your child's or children's schools.

___ Ministers or priests can openly talk about the threats of sexual abuse to their adult congregations and design lesson/sermon plans that include open discussions on protection.

___ Teachers of older children and teenagers can design lesson plans on sexual abuse prevention and use them in health classes. The lessons could include self-protection strategies.

___ Teachers of very young children can read out loud to their students books that increase self-awareness and self-esteem. Although I mentioned earlier some children's books that I believe increase children's self-esteem, others also include Mercer and Gina Mayer's *JUST LOST,* which is a book about a little critter getting lost and finding his mother through safe channels. It is a book that empowers the very young. Other books by Mercer Mayer that increase self-esteem are *I WAS SO MAD* and *ALL BY MYSELF.*

{ Although these books do not discuss sexual abuse prevention, they do increase the self-esteems of children -- empowering them to take control when or if they find themselves in trouble. They teach self-reliance and illustrate that feelings -- feeling angry is not wrong because it is part of our human emotions. Offenders or potential offenders do not normally target children who appear in control and well-esteemed -- children who might make a scene, yell, run and alert responsible adults. }

__ Encouraging and helping children select proper and age appropriate reading materials, computer programs and videos is another suggestion.

__ Encourage and praise school and home activities that build self-confidence and healthy esteem in children (dance - ballet, tap, jazz; self-defense classes; sports - swimming, tennis, gymnastics, running, basketball; music - voice, etc.)

In *Chapter III: Sexual Offenders: Who Are They?* sexually deviant behavior in terms of child abuse is defined, categorized, and discussed at length in personal interviews and excerpts. More details are provided in an appendix.

One of the purposes of including the following chapter is to give survivors and those whose sincerity is with or without them, the understanding that sexual abuse is solely perpetrated, caused by and is the exclusive transgression of the offender. Both those victimized and those never touched by such victimization look for logical evidence that proves to others that the victims did not ask to be assaulted. Survivors sometimes find themselves searching for evidence outside their own experiences, to justify their accusations to any doubting listeners.

Victims and survivors know they did not ask to be assaulted, but they are keenly aware that others will cast doubt on their claims. Although most of us understand logically that no one -- particularly children, asked for abusive treatment, we hear cons and alibis surrounding child rape victims in the media true life court cases and in fiction, and it becomes arduous in deciphering truth from fabrication. I hope that you are still with me.

Offenders can be stopped -- no matter who they are and no matter what other roles they have played in victims' lives. They can even be stopped before they have offended by empowering, as I pointed out earlier, our children (and ourselves) with knowledge and healthy self-esteems.

I believe that offenders are molded and primed by the experiences they have during childhood. They begin as innocents -- soon touched by the products of dysfunctional families and society. The quality of life for every child -- *every* baby at *every* stage of emotional and physical development needs to be *everyone's* concern.

Because this is an emotionally challenging topic, I have taken measures to spare readers from the most grotesque details and accounts of sexual abuse I have come across during the interviewing process. Because our aim is prevention, I have included necessary accounts illustrative of the sort of scenarios common among the sexually abused. Accounts often render solutions when problems are out front. If your child's arm gets broken, his or her cries and words point you in the right direction to the problem. When you understand the problem, you are able to render the correct solution and possible safety tips for preventing it from occurring again. The same can be done to prevent child sexual abuse crimes. Read on.

CHAPTER

"Do not be deceived: God cannot be mocked. A man reaps what he sows. The one who sows to please his sinful nature, from that nature will reap destruction; the one who sows to please the Spirit, from the Spirit will reap eternal life." -- Galatians 6:07, 8. *(NIV)*.

Sex Offenders -- Who Are They?

What Can We Learn From Offenders?

In terms of prevention, what can we use from the information obtained about sex offenders? As mentioned in earlier chapters, we can learn the sort of settings and opportunities offenders take advantage of in order to offend. Understanding facts and truths about sexual offenders makes them real to non-victims and to those disbelieving ones who doubt the severity and extent of such crimes.

According to statistics compiled by The National Center On Child Abuse Prevention Research, a program of The National Committee to Prevent Child Abuse (NCPCA), a 1996 fifty state survey reveals that an estimated 969,000 children were substantiated by child protective service agencies as victims of maltreatment and nine percent of these represented confirmed sexual abuse cases.* Furthermore, the NCPCA reports that studies of the general adult population reveal anywhere between six and 63 percent of females were sexually abused as children.*

It is fair to speculate that many acts of sexual abuse towards children go unreported and many suffer in silence even after the abuse stops. Men who are sexually abused as children are less likely than females to step forward to report having been sexually abused, but when they do, this is achieved with great difficulty due to serious fears of possible alienation from loved ones and friends.

Still, some researchers report that the typical child sex offender molests an average of 117 children before being stopped, and most of the victims do not report the offenses. This emphasizes warnings for stronger preventative steps, and these are beckoning with the utmost urgency.

What can we learn in terms of prevention by reading the confessions of sexual offenders? We discover that most all offenders were abused in some way as children -- either sexually, physically or emotionally or in every way possible. Prevention's goal should include motivating parents, guardians or caretakers to reassess their parenting techniques and skills and to seek information on what constitutes discipline versus abuse and to seek serious help for drug and alcohol addictions and/or counseling to come to terms with past childhood traumas or abuse.

Nevertheless, our society has always managed to put on fronts to hide its problems or color them or pretend they are not as bad as some claim or to sensationalize the lives of those who are victimized or to sensationalize the topic of sexual abuse in general. Sensationalism incites another sort of poison hype. It destroys the faith and hope for consistent protection and normalcy. Sensationalism is like mania. When it slopes into a media depression, doubt (in regard to the real truths of some sexual abuse stories) triggers the birth pains for another "*sensational*" angle. It's a terribly sad fact that some would rather allow our innocents, our world's children; to suffer and bear it or stuff it, than aggressively unravel the knots of our social and familial dysfunctions.

As you read the interviews, note the circumstances that the offenders developed in as children themselves while growing up. It appears that the dysfunctional upbringings of the offenders blew up in the faces of children and then the court system. It is a shameful way of life, and it is much easier to criticize than it is to first understand the entire process of dysfunctional behavior.

It is much easier for us to distance and separate ourselves than take responsibility for influences society and families have over some individuals. Some learn to cope with past childhood traumas and dysfunctional humiliations at the hands of childhood caretakers by using drugs and alcohol and/or seeking relations with others who have the same or worse upbringings. All of this looking into the cribs of babies who are subjected to their caretakers' worlds is a frightening reality.

Through the offenders' interviews, we learn the opportunities and places they took advantage of in order to commit their crimes. The interviews help us to realize the seriousness of child sexual abuse. We learn how vulnerable we all are to the influences of an abusive society. We are moved to see what we as individuals can do to prevent it. At the end of this chapter, you will find a prevention checklist. Use this and the others provided in this book to help you design your own personalized plan to prevent sexual abuse.

Taking A Closer Look At Society

The dysfunctional themes immersed in the American culture and other cultures as well, may make it easier for citizens to ignore or disregard or discredit claims of child sexual abuse. We need to take a closer look at how we operate as a society -- politically, religiously, commercially and artistically and take responsible actions within these areas in protecting our children and ourselves. We do this by not allowing the sexual exploitations of any human being to be used for entertainment or monetary gain of any sort. Sexual offenders use children to entertain themselves and to materialize immoral and sometimes nefarious fantasies.

If we consider the sorts of influences that are immersed into our daily living in some movies and advertisements, it is not surprising that there are people who still doubt the claims of children or the extent of them. It is difficult to see innocence clearly when our own vulnerabilities to erotic idolatry has already been carved and bought without even a second thought.

The erotic rubbish allowed in our society to influence our decisions about the clothes we wear to the food we eat piled on top of alcoholism or drug addictions and/or the suppressed rage of a wronged child in the body of an adult molds toxic interpretations on how we should live and what offensive behavior actually is. Toxic outlooks give birth to toxic opinions -- opinions based on false information presented as true. Children being raised in the midst of such toxicity is like putting trust in a stone to mend a wound. So, where do we begin with offenders?

Appearances Can Be Deceiving

Perpetrators of child molestation do not have a certain appearance about them. Characteristics of their behavior, however, sew common threads of familial and social dysfunctional patterns, which are seen in the accounts later in this chapter. Attempting to categorize people who are sexually deviant in one way or another has been the focus of some researchers.

During my search to understand offenders -- their behavior patterns, childhood experiences, etc., I came across research that categorizes offenders into types. Categorizing offenders can be helpful in understanding what we as a society must face up to. Sexual offenders are often real products of our society, our families.

Some researchers divide sex offenders, who are often referred to as pedophiles, into three categories. For example: immature, regressed and aggressive. Curt R. and Anne M. Bartol discuss personality offender types in *Criminal Behavior, A Psychosocial Approach.* For instance, the immature child molester has never developed mature relationships with adults. The immature child molester is considered socially immature, passive and dependent. The extent of his crimes is usually limited to sexual acts that involve touching, fondling, caressing, tasting and smelling. The immature offender seeks children out as sexual companions, and his or her wishes usually materialize after the child has gotten to know them over a period of time.

The regressed child molester usually has problems in his/ her job, and in sexual and social relationships with adults. The regressed offender had relatively normal teenage years, good peer heterosexual experiences; however, he later developed feelings of masculine inadequacy and self-doubt. The background of a regressed offender may include alcoholism, divorce and poor employment histories, but nevertheless, his lifestyle and circumstances are stressful. The victims of such perpetrators are often female. Regressed offenders, according to other researchers, begin to offend as they seek to return to feelings they had in less threatening times of their lives. They *regress*. They turn to children, and use them as substitutes for their adult needs. The relationships regressed offenders seek with children are usually very *unfulfilling* for the offenders and unquestionably damaging for the victims.

The aggressive child sexual offender, as discussed by the Bartols in *Criminal Behavior,* is attracted to children for both sexual and aggressive motives. The aggressive child molester's background likely includes a history of antisocial behavior. According to the Bartols, aggressive child sexual offenders often assault children *"viciously and sadistically ... The more harm and pain inflicted, the more this offender becomes sexually excited."* * The aggressive child sexual offender is most responsible for child abductions and murders.

{Research by others suggests additionally that sexual abuse is a form of temporary abduction. Offenders keep victims away from anyone who could possibly defend them until the offender decides he or she is finished with them.}

An interesting and valuable point the Bartols make in their book is that the behavior of aggressive child sexual offenders resembles psychopathic behavior. The Bartols point out that aggressive child sexual offenders are rare "*and might be better labeled psychopathic child offenders.*" * Psychopaths are often seen as charming and intelligent; however, they appear to lack morals and genuine concern and sensitivity for others. When a psychopath participates in criminal acts, his or her crimes are done without any seemingly rational motives. The psychopath is not capable of remorse. Not all psychopaths are criminals.

Who Do Offenders Seek As Victims?

A given sexual offender may have a preference for a child of a specific age and gender, and even a particular coloring or type of physique. Some want only immature children, while others are attracted to pubescent or young adolescent boys or girls. Given the diversity of offender preferences, no child or adolescent is immune from the risk of molestation. Ironically, a child is more at risk from a friend than a stranger; the perpetrator makes a point of getting to know his or her intended victim, gaining the trust of a child's parent as well.

The Bartols report in *Criminal Behavior:*

"**.... Many victims were actively seeking natural affection from their offenders, as a child seeks to be hugged or cuddled. Some victims feel kindly and lovingly toward the offender, who sometimes interprets this behavior as "seductive." It is not uncommon for the sexual behavior between the offender and victim to have gone on for a sustained period of time.**" *
{ **Source:** *Criminal Behavior, A Psychosocial Approach* **by Curt R. Bartol and Anne M. Bartol. Copyright (c) 1986 by Prentice-Hall, a Division of Simon & Schuster, Inc. Reprinted with permission of the publisher.** }

122

Portrait Of A Sex Offender

While researching and writing *Shielding Our Innocents,* I came across many portraits of sexual offenders. Descriptions often overlaped; however, many included the following details:

1) Reported or known child sex offenders are nearly always male.

2) Some child sex offenders begin molesting or assaulting during their adolescent years.

3) The sex offender can molest hundreds of youngsters before being stopped. In cases of incest, some offenders molest only one or two.

4) Offenders engage in a variety of deviant sexual behaviors.

5) Offenders are likely to know their victims.

6) Offenders were often victimized emotionally and/or physically as children.

The Idaho Department of Law Enforcement Statistical Analysis Center quoted researcher Dr. Gene G. Abel in *CHILD ABUSE IN IDAHO: THE PROBLEM, ITS IMPACT, AND A PERSPECTIVE FOR CHANGE,* as saying:

"Everyone is so surprised that a priest is a child molester, or that a school teacher is a child molester .... I am flabbergasted that anyone would be surprised. Child molesters select jobs to access kids. That's why they become pediatricians, child psychiatrists and they work in boy's camps in the summer." *
{ Source: Quoted with permission from Gene G. Abel, M.D. 5-29-97. }

Perpetrators of sexual abuse may involve incestuous relationships between fathers (or stepfathers) and their daughters or sons. Grandfathers and uncles may sexually abuse granddaughters and nieces. (Interviews illustrative of sexual abuse situations can be found in *Chapter II: Individual Recollections From Adult Survivors.*) Stepfathers and baby-sitters are reported for sexually abusing children, and seen in news reports on court cases across the United States and throughout the globe. In regard to incest between siblings, the Idaho report points out that this sort of abuse is widespread and seldomly reported. "*... the stranger abuses a particular child only one time but will continue to abuse other children.*" *

Typical male sex offenders are passive, have low self-esteem and look down on other sex offenders. Sex offenders, according to interviews I have included in this chapter, grew up learning to be passive, while being emotionally or physically abused at home or at school by peers. Most of the offenders I interviewed reported growing up in dysfunctional family environments and had poor or absent relationships with their parents. Some offenders I interviewed during the research phases of this book were raised in households that included abusive step-parents and in environments that were not emotionally safe.

According to Lucy Berliner and Doris Stevens in "CLINICAL ISSUES IN CHILD SEXUAL ABUSE," a chapter of the *Journal of Social Work & Human Sexuality*, Vol. 1, 1982 / 83, child molesters are characteristically self-centered, insecure and immature men. These men have difficulty with interpersonal relationships.

"Many of them were physically or sexually abused as children or grew up in a home in which there was abuse toward others ... certain personality characteristics (such as shyness, inadequacies, lack of confidence), in

124

combination with childhood experiences (e.g. sexual or physical abuse) and/or situational factors (e.g. loss of job, other stresses) can lead to a pattern of sexual offending against a child. The pattern begins in adolescence for many offenders ... Becoming a sexual offender does not occur suddenly. It is a gradual process, beginning with thoughts and fantasies (elaborate mental scenarios about sexual encounters) and finally leading to the actual commission of the act ... Since the offender knows it is wrong to molest a child, he rationalizes the behavior by calling it something else (e.g., "sex education"), by blaming external factors ("I was drinking"; "she wanted it"; "my wife turned me down"), or by minimizing the extent or impact ("it was only a few times"; "it didn't hurt her"). This cognitive distortion allows for repetition of the offending behavior, which almost always continues until it is interrupted by some outside force: disclosure, or no available victim..." *

{ Source: *Journal of Social Work & Human Sexuality*, "*CLINICAL ISSUES IN CHILD SEXUAL ABUSE*" by Lucy Berliner and Doris Stevens. Copyright (c) 1982, The Haworth Press, Inc. Reprinted with permission of the publisher. }

To better understand the framework of a child molester, it is necessary to consider what Jon R. Conte in his book, *A Look at Child Sexual Abuse,* refers to as six clinical aspects of the sexual abuser: Denial, sexual arousal, sexual fantasy, social skills, cognitive distortions and other psychological and social problems. A child molester -- like other people with deviant behaviors, is not going to want to volunteer any information that would bring his/her illegal and immoral behaviors into the limelight and socially stigmatize his/her existence. People who molest or sexually abuse children know that this kind of behavior is not accepted and is actively frowned upon by courts and other law enforcements. The child molester may rationalize his actions by telling himself, "*She won't remember. She is too young.*" or "*She asked for it. She enjoyed it. What could it hurt?*"

It is possible that some molesters have denied their actions for so long they have developed a sort of selected amnesia. Some researchers measure a molester's sexual arousal to children. For example, researcher and writer Jon R. Conte cited such a measurement.

"... Abel and colleagues were able correctly to identify child molesters who had been more violent in their abuse of children by comparing sexual arousal to imagined scenes depicting violence against children with imagined scenes without violence. More violent child molesters showed greater sexual arousal in the laboratory to scenes with violent content." *
{ Source: *A Look at Child Sexual Abuse* **by Jon R. Conte. Copyright (c) 1986 by National Committee to Prevent Child Abuse. All Rights Reserved. Reprinted with permission of publisher. }**

Sexual fantasy material of the molester may be discussed and examined during therapy sessions or counseling. Getting the abuser or child sex offender to talk about his fantasies may help him to acknowledge past deviant behaviors. The abuser may have cognitively distorted his/her experiences with children. He/she may minimize what he/she has done, saying to himself/herself that the child never resisted, so she/he must have wanted it. The molester may also tell himself/herself that having sex with children is not really a sexual problem or feel that touching and fondling is not abuse because he/she did not have intercourse. The child molester may have a history of other psychological problems, including alcoholism and drug abuse, feelings of inadequacy, depression, inability to control his impulses and a poor self-concept.

"It is not at all clear that adults have sex with children because they are depressed, or have poor self-concepts," * Conte writes. *"Perhaps they are depressed or have poor self-concepts because they sexually abuse children."* * **{ Source:** *A Look at Child Sexual Abuse* **by Jon R. Conte. Copyright (c) 1986 by National Committee to Prevent Child Abuse. All Rights Reserved. Reprinted with permission from the publisher.}**

Another aspect to consider is that the child molester may lack appropriate social skills. He may feel more socially accepted in the presence of children than in the presence of adults. Getting a clearer picture of the sexual offender -- who the offender targets to victimize, where the offender gains access to potential victims and what the offender depends on to remain hidden from authorities can help us design a prevention plan. Different lifestyles and stages of life will have some influence on how we as individuals decide to take personal steps to protect our children -- future adults, from having to suffer.

The following accounts were emotionally difficult for me to digest -- to sit and listen, note and audio tape the candid confessions. Although their crimes are horrendously shameful, many of the offenders I spoke with are coming to terms with themselves -- holding themselves accountable for their actions. Their accounts should be understood as words of warning for the unsuspecting and seriously by unbelievers. The confessions of the sexual offenders *confirm* the stories of serious circumstances that have been ignored or discredited by others. It is shameful if we go to sleep at night without even praying for children unknown to us who are enduring abuses behind doors we never see until its too late or if we ever see or hear of them at all.

As you read this book, many children are being born -- completely innocent, unmarked of feeling shame of having been sexually abused. And today, as you read this book, little children suffer at the hands and efforts of those we can stop.

Accounts From Sexual Offenders

The following accounts are from offenders who found opportunities to abuse children. These interviews comprise two regressed offenders who opportunistically engaged themselves into deviant sexual acts with children. The offenders here, like others, suffered or have suffered from alcohol and/or drug abuse and/or depression. They are remorseful, as they often are, for engaging themselves in sexual acts with children.

{A second type of opportunistic or regressed offender is called the sexually indiscriminate. These offenders are not motivated by conquest like the morally indiscriminate, according to Tyson. (See the *Appendix for Chapter III*.) They lack judgment, morals and cannot understand why there should be any interference with what they did.}

The third interview in this chapter contains the confessions of a pedophile -- who intellectually recognizes his actions as wrong and harmful in the eyes of society. His confession reveals, however, that he does not truly recognize the real indecency of his crimes and how his actions will affect his victims later in life. He distorts his understanding of his actions as being part of the love he claims to have for those he victimized.

Identities of all sex offenders who consented to interviews are held in confidence. The offenders agreed to share their stories in order to meet the objectives of this book. (See the *appendix* for additional information on offenders.)

Accounts From Sexual Offenders
(In Active Therapy)

Account From Man Who Sexually Abused His Daughter

Background:

The following account is from a 34-year-old sex offender. The offender is currently participating in group therapy -- having pleaded guilty to two counts of taking indecent liberties with his 9-year-old daughter. The offender was placed on probation with a special condition of probation that requires he participate in group therapy for sex offenders.

At the time of this interview in 1990, he was informed that if he violated his probation in any fashion, he could activate his 5-year sentence, which was suspended initially in Superior Court. He is a college graduate, divorced from two marriages and the father of two children.

Aside from group therapy, he has received some family counseling. This therapy, however, took place before he molested his daughter. In addition to group therapy, he has received some individual counseling sessions from a psychologist who specializes in the treatment and rehabilitation of sex offenders.

His Story Of The Abuse

"I abused my daughter on September tenth, 1988, I believe ... I performed oral sex on my daughter. This was the first time I ever did that. I had this weird idea in my head that I could take the genital area -- the boobs and bottom and draw little circles around them. Everything else was free to do little back scratches, to tickle and play with. When my daughter would be in close physical contact with me, I would get aroused or something like that. If you really want to be honest about it, it was a progression.

"In the beginning, I told myself, my daughter's private parts were off limits ... I have never had a decent relationship with any woman I have been associated with in my life.

"My daughter was very loving, kind and affectionate with me. Me and how my fantasy world developed is how I wanted a woman to treat me ... I just let things go crazy in my head. My wife did not give me the same affection and attention my daughter did.

"My wife and I had long, one-sided conversations about how indecent I was and what a piece of s--- I was ... The first transition of the abuse that involved my daughter actually began when we would be walking around the house in our underwear.

"*I would catch my children staring at my crotch. I know that children are naturally curious. It is pretty difficult dealing with what I did. It's scary.*

"*The thing with my daughter was like meeting someone and dating them. You know, the longer you think about a certain someone, the more intimate the touching may become ... Before I performed oral sex on her, her genitals had always been off limits to me until that day.*

"*...She just came in the door. I conditioned her to respond to me in certain ways. I always thought that she was this little part of my head ... like she knew what I was doing, and she liked it too. This, I know now, is just a bunch of s---. I was just trying to make me happy.*

"*She came in one Saturday morning. I had a headache. She came in and just plopped right on top of my stomach. I just took it a little too far. I tickled her ribs and scratched her back. She was free with her body, which is fine if my head would have been okay, but it was not.*

"*She would always make the point to be in close physical contact with me because she knew I liked it, and I needed that at the time ... There was a lot of drinking. I smoked a lot of pot. I don't drink like that anymore. I am trying to take better care of myself because I am finally beginning to like myself...*

"*I was involved in therapy before the specific act of sexual abuse that I was charged with. It was family-related therapy ... about sexual abuse. I had my kids and sued for custody back in 1984. They had been through a lot. My son had been sexually abused by a stepfather and was forced to perform oral sex ... He also had some stuff done directly to him ... My second marriage slowly turned sour...*"

"My wife was antagonistic, and there were arguments and spankings. I used to travel a lot in sales. I would come home to a hell hole....

"I was passive ... the typical passive aggressor, had a low self-esteem. I just let things roll along, telling myself that things were going to get better. We went to a church counselor to ask what to do about the family, and he recommended someone. We started going to him in the spring of 1987.

"He (the therapist) immediately identified my wife as being extremely depressed. This really freaked her out, so then it was just me going to counseling. Then, I started taking my son, who was this 'supposed' victim. It is really strange looking back.

"... This is really strange because my thinking started getting messed up about that time. I am not blaming this on the therapist. When I started going to see him, I just felt like s---. My wife would scream and beat on me when we came out of there. Sometimes, I think if I had had a therapist like the one I have now, my family would have had a chance."

His Own Childhood

"From what I can remember, I did not experience direct sexual abuse ... My mother is still alive. My mother is one of these ragers, okay. She is very dominating ... She screamed and hollered a lot when I was a little boy. She called me a little bastard ... I began to think I was illegitimate ... She did things to my older sister too, but my sister always realized that our mother was a little strange, and I never did. I thought this was how everyone's mother was ... My father was not abusive. He would just be the one to come in and do the punishing. My mother would smack me around and hit me in the head, and then tell me my father was going to punish me when he got home. He just did what she said.

"He was passive. She let him know what she wanted out of life right away, and that she wanted this or that followed to a T. When men touch her or hug her, she freezes up. She's cold. I just never could please the woman. I spent all my life trying to.

" .... She used to take naps when I was in preschool. I could not make any noise. She was nit-picky. The biggest thing I ever did wrong is when I was going through puberty. If I had a wet dream, there would be emissions on my shorts. When she would wash them, she found them. The stains would be set in.

"She would ask me, 'Have you been doing this?' I would tearfully admit that I had ... Then, she would be after me with questions all the time, like how long it took me to go to the bathroom or to take a bath or did I splash water while I was bathing because this could mean that I was masturbating.

"...She punished me for doing things like this. I really forget how she punished me all the time. All I basically remember is that I had to talk to my dad about it, and I was made to feel like s---. It was getting to the point where I was getting older.

"The physical part, the slapping, had kind of faded out. My father would always back her up. He made me feel bad, like I was doing something horrible. It took me a long time to realize that it is okay to have a pleasure orgasm. That it was okay, and the devil was not going to get me..."

"But, she would give me these stories that my testicles were going to grow to the size of grapefruits, and that I was going to end up in an insane asylum just masturbating all day long ... I did not really know if she was handing me a line or what. I was raised on a farm, where I did not have anybody to talk to.

" .... I think that one thing that really trashed me out, as far as my self-esteem and male ego are concerned, is when I was going through puberty. I started getting knots in my breasts. This freaked me out. I thought I was going to grow breasts like a girl ... So, I told my mother about it. She claimed it was from masturbation. All I know is that I was embarrassed to talk about it. I found out later after graduating from high school and taking a physical for college that it was normal ....

"I had no privacy ... absolutely none. She busted in on me one time. She did not catch me masturbating under the covers, but you can't hide an erection ... She made me strip off and put on one of my sister's bras and just sit there in front of them ... in front of both my parents ... I guess I was going to have big breasts, big testicles and be in an insane asylum. You know, this really just totally trashed me out. I was utterly humiliated having to sit there wearing my sister's bra."

"... If someone had just pulled me off to the side and said, 'Wait a minute guy. This is very messed up.' That's what I needed, but there wasn't anybody. I was about eleven or maybe twelve when she did this to me. I reached puberty fairly early. I'll say the sixth grade.

" .... After that, I would always try to go for the unattainable as far as girls were concerned ... I felt like I was not good enough. I believed I was a piece of s----.

"...But, I made great grades. I got scholarships. I was really firmly and emotionally attached to home despite all these things. I would come home from college."

His Conclusions

"My mother nearly died when I was born, and she would tell me about it. I would feel terrible ... I wish someone had got to me before I molested my daughter ... I sit and think about what I did every day ... I am digging more to the past, talking to my sister and trying to understand what happened. I had one meeting with my daughter and counselor to talk about it ... but we really did not get to the meat of the situation.

"I still want to be a father to my daughter ... But, now my daughter has something over me. I still feel the same way toward my kids when I sued for custody. I am really the only one to stand up for them. They are not in my custody now. They are with foster parents with the Department of Social Services.

" .... When I was in the courtroom, I felt, 'Well, you really messed things up this time.' My daughter was in my care a month after she told about the molestation. I did not try to coerce her into retracting or not telling. All I said was, 'Look at what you are doing. This is family right here.' I did not try to talk her out of telling what happened, but I was afraid. I pleaded guilty to having oral sex with her and for playing with her breasts. I used to pray to God about it ...."

"*Since then, I have written one letter to my daughter and one to my son with the help of my psychologist ... This whole thing has been going on with social services for two years now. The Department of Social Services has not even began addressing my children's issues and problems in dealing with their father -- me. I think this is ludicrous.*

"*.... It seems that the concept of me being a parent for my children gets dimmer and dimmer. This really upsets me. We already have enough victimization in this case. Let's don't make it any worse. It's like if I shot one of my kids. Authorities would haul me off to rehabilitation and leave my children there to bleed -- removed from me.*

" *... If they don't watch it, they are going to make my daughter the ultimate victim. She is going to go out and act like this marked person. She is going to think she can explain anything that is wrong because she is this marked person. She is far too intelligent, and has too much going for her to be treated this way. I have sat there and watched her therapist putting words into her mouth: 'Well, you feel this way ... don't you?' I mean, give me a break.*

"*My kids know me. They know I am dad. There is plenty I have to make up for -- plenty of repairs to do, but they know that I am not going to sit there and beat the hell out of them ... I am allowed to call my son on the telephone, but I am not allowed to talk to or see my daughter.*

"*I send my children support checks. My daughter endorsed one of the checks. On the back, she wrote, 'Hi, Dad. Thanks a lot.' She is a great kid. I really hate to see the ineptness of the system ... The sexual abuse is in the past now. Let's do something positive with our lives.*"

136

Where's Mother?

In regard to where the natural mother is and what her place has been throughout the ordeal, the offender said he was not too sure where she lives. "The last I spoke with her was in August 1988."

Account From Homemaker (Survivor) Turned Offender

Background:

The following account is from a 20-year-old female sex offender. The woman was convicted in Superior Court of one count of taking indecent liberties with her 5-year-old niece. The woman was placed on probation for five years after receiving a suspended 10-year sentence. At the time of this interview, she had participated in group therapy for two months. Continued group therapy is a special condition of her probation. (Other conditions of her probation include having no contact with the victim or the victim's mother.)

Aside from group therapy, the woman says she participated in one session of family therapy at age 11. She says as a student, she had difficulty concentrating in school, skipped classes and did not care about school in general. Past occupations include working as a cashier. According to information obtained in a personal interview, the woman left home at age 15 and started supporting herself at age 16 -- a year after she dropped out of high school.

She is married and is not employed outside the home. She cares for her newborn infant. Her story begins with her own recollections of being sexually abused between the ages of nine and 13 by her stepfather.

Her Own Victimization

As A Child And Teenager

"My mom worked at the time, and he did not. My stepfather was around twenty-five years old then. I have brothers and sisters, but he did not sexually abuse them that I know of. I guess because I sat on his lap he thought he could do what he did to me.

"After my mom had gone to work, he would get me on the ground and start unbuttoning my shirt. He attempted to do something else. He started touching my breasts. He tried to unzip my jeans -- but I was able to stop him. One day we were sitting at the dinner table, and I told my mom about it right in front of him. He denied it in front of her.

"My mom called me a liar and believed him over me. That kind of destroyed me and my trust in my mother protecting me. He did not try anything after this. I had so much hatred toward him. I did not treat him like a stepfather. I would not let him come close to me. He was the type of person that if he punished me, he used something like a plastic baseball bat or a belt on my bare bottom.

"One time he asked me not to ask my mama about something because I wanted to go out with a neighbor some place.

"I walked into the bathroom where my mom was. She was putting make-up on. He said, 'I told you no.' He was going to lock me in the bathroom. I ran into the bedroom. I told him he was not my real daddy, and he could not hit me. That's when I left home. He took my mom to work. I packed some of my things and left. He had hit me earlier that day with his hand on my arm. I remember it hurting. I was afraid of him, but I did not think of it. I just wanted out. He is about thirty-one years old now.

"The reason I never went to court about him sexually abusing me is that he helps my mother financially. He helps support my brother who is blind and mentally retarded. That's the only reason I have not done anything. I still think about taking him to court now, but I think it's too late .... I think he hits my mom. He also hits my brother. He ties him to the commode, so he won't get up. They say he misuses the commode. My stepfather yells at my brother like a dog.

"I have never confronted my stepfather about what he did to me. I bring it up to my mother now and then. She will say, 'Oh, you still think he did that.' She still denies it. She denies it to herself, but I think she knows it's true.

"I am not afraid of my stepfather now. If I had the guts to talk to him about what he did to me and how it has hurt me, I would tell him he screwed up my life because I turned around and did the same thing ... I would like to confront him in front of my mom just to make him look terrible because he made me feel terrible ... I know his actions will catch up to him sooner or later."

Her Story About Offending

"I was nineteen years old when I sexually offended my husband's sister's little girl. The girl was five years old. There was a lot of stuff going on in my life then ... There were drugs around. Cocaine, I started doing that. It was the first time I ever used it. It kind of screwed with my mind. It probably brought me back to the time my stepfather did it to me. It made my mind not work right. That's the way I look at it.

"I do not know what I was thinking at the time, but we were there sitting on the bed watching television one morning. I touched her on the outside of her panties. She told her mommy about it. That's all that happened.

"What kind of got to me is that they said I did worse because she was red down there. I gave her a bath the night before. I was trying to wash her. I was not thinking about touching her then. I was just trying to wash her down there because her mama never taught her how. My niece kept backing up from me like I was hurting her, and this kind of made me think about what had happened.

"The way I look at it is that she was touched internally. They (legal authorities) think I did that -- but I didn't. I was trying to wash her, and I guess it hurt her down there. She backed up from me like I was hurting her. I didn't see any blood on her. Her tissues were red. She didn't say anything. She just backed up to the corner of the bathtub. I said, 'Well, here's the washrag. Do it yourself,' and I walked out of the bathroom.

"I think the cocaine had a lot to do with the fact that I touched her at all. My niece told her cousin. Her other aunt heard her talking and asked her to come inside and explain. The next thing I knew is her mother called that evening after she had returned home. Her mother asked me if I had touched her. I told her, 'No,' of course. I don't think I would have done it had I not been on cocaine. The cocaine brought back bad memories to me. I thought, I guess, that since my stepfather got away with it, then I would, but I didn't.

"They (legal authorities) say I went inside her because her tissues were torn and red. They were like that when I gave her a bath. I never went inside her panties.

" .... My husband said his sister's new husband's little boy came up to him and asked him what it is exactly boys and girls do in bed. My husband turned around and told him it was not his place to say things like that, and even if it was, he would not tell him.

"I think that little boy had something to do with it ... I think someone I know touched her. I think it could have been my niece's stepbrother. He is eleven years old. This all happened after he asked my husband that question. My niece's siblings all sleep in the same bed together."

Her Conclusions

"I knew I did something wrong. I still deny it to certain people because I do not want them to know what is going on ... like my mom. I am glad I got stopped and helped. I hope others will get help as well. After it happened, I told my husband. He was disappointed, but I was glad I opened up to him."

Account From School Teacher Who Abused A Student

Background:

The following account is from a 44-year-old man who pleaded guilty to two counts of taking indecent liberties with a child. (He was originally charged with four counts of taking indecent liberties with a child, but two counts were dropped during a plea arrangement between the State and the defendant. This offender received a suspended 5-year sentence and was placed on probation for five years with special conditions. Special conditions include that he participate in regular group therapy for sex offenders. This man is a former school teacher for children grades four through nine. He currently works as an artist.

He is a college graduate, divorced with no children. He has participated in group therapy for the past three years. Part of his therapy has included three months of individual counseling. The offender says he was emotionally abused as a child by a teacher and other school children.

He explains that he was often severely teased because of a birth defect. (The offender's birth defect cannot be named due to his request.) The victim he was prosecuted on behalf of was a 12-year-old boy. (The offender admits that he sexually abused another boy prior to this molestation, but legal action was not taken against him for prior offenses.)

142

His Story

"It happened when I worked with emotionally and behavioral problem children. I was a counselor and had to take care of children ages ten to twelve years old. I was in charge of feeding them and taking care of them in general. Some of the children had emotional behavior type problems.

"We (victim and himself) developed a relationship after he left the center. He was twelve years old at the time. He had been in the center because of behavior problems. His parents could not control him. We became kind of drawn to each other. He wanted a lot of attention. All of them did, but he seemed to get upset if I did not pay him enough attention.

"When I put the kids to bed, he always asked me to stay with him. He would say, 'Stay and talk to me or lay next to me.' He just demanded all the attention I could give. We would sleep in the same bed a lot together because that is what he wanted. I would tell him I couldn't because of my responsibilities to the other kids. He would get upset and throw a tantrum and say, 'I am not going to sleep unless you sit here beside me.' He was pretty powerful. I enjoyed having his company. He was in my care for three to four months.

"When he left to go back to his adoptive parents, he called me once a week. We got to see each other. He was always calling me and asking me to come see him. I would drive up to see him.

"We spent two weekends at his parents' campsite. He was never afraid of me, and I never threatened him. It just kind of took its own course ... We talked a lot and wrote letters. His adoptive mother found a letter and started questioning him about it and what we did together. He started telling her some things. Then, she went back to where I was working. She told the authorities at the center. They informed the Department of Social Services. The parents came in and spoke with the director of the center. They asked me about it. It ended up that I had to quit my job. This happened in November. I did not get arrested and charged until January.

"I did not hurt him. There was a lot of hugging and kissing. But, there was more fondling. He never sexually touched me. He just always wanted a hug or a kiss. I kissed him on the mouth. I took him to movies and arcades. So, there were a lot of good relations between us overall. But, most of it -- the abuse, I tried to do while he was asleep. I would touch him while he was a sleep.

"I never had intercourse with him. It was mostly, like I say, hugging, kissing and fondling. I did most of the touching while he was asleep, but apparently he was not asleep. I would tell him if I said or did anything that he did not like or want to just tell me. He would say, 'Everything is just fine.' I kept trying to talk with him about what was happening.

"He did not seem nervous. He still enjoyed being with me. I guess he still enjoyed being with me even though certain things were happening. I guess for him some attention was better than no attention.

"The Department of Social Services and the courts will not allow me to have any contact with the boy. I wrote a letter to him and his parents. I apologized for misusing their trust and for not really talking to them. I told them if there was anything I could do or if they ever wanted to sit down and discuss it ....

"This boy, as I said before, had been adopted at an early age. I was real close to one of his relatives. One relative of his would always run up to me for a hug. I would try to keep cool because of what was happening with the first child. So, I did have certain controls.

"I feel sorry for misusing the friendship. He really needed somebody. He is the only boy I had ever gotten this involved with. There was another boy I molested. I touched a thirteen year old boy when I was thirty-five years old. I really cared for the twelve-year-old, however.

"I guess we have different strengths and weaknesses. I have had plenty of long relationships with kids. As far as adult females, I have the same interest. I do not consider myself homosexual.

"It is not that I could not be happy with a woman ... When I have sought relationships, I ended up with a woman who cheated on me because she thought that I was starting to get like her 'old husband.' She really did not give it a chance. She was thirty-four, and I was thirty-three ... Most of the relationships I have had with women have been disastrous."

How He Feels About Sexually Abused Children, Their Offenders and Himself

(This offender said although he had only touched two boys, he had thought about touching other children who were in his care or who lived close to him. He said he had never touched or thought about touching relatives of his who were children.)

"If I had a child and someone touched him in a sexual manner I would be upset. I would probably choke him ... This is difficult to say because of who I am. If a person violates a child, it is natural to get upset. I understand how someone could feel toward me. I have to sort things out.

"I have sat around and heard people talking about things like this -- my situation. They say, 'Can you imagine someone doing something like this to a child?' Of course I say, 'No, I can't imagine.' And, of course, I am in the same situation, yet I still have a hard time knowing who I am and how things are, and yet I see other things -- How, for example, could a person kidnap a kid and threaten his life? I could never do this. I could never hurt a kid. To actually physically hurt a kid, I could never do this .... To me, this is sick. I know that I am sick, but this kind of violence is really sick. I am sick, but I am not evil. Society sees this kind of sex offender -- the physically violent kind, in the same way it sees me. But, we are not the same. I would like to go on television, hide my face and say this is how it is ....

"The boy needs to know that I am sorry for what I did and that I really cared for him. It bothers me that I don't know how he has dealt with it ... I see childrens' needs. This is what draws me near to them. Then, something in my head just goes haywire. I do love the boy aside from anything sexual ... I was not really confused. I know the boy wanted acceptance ... I get attached to people. We were close. We had a lot of contact.

"He (his victim) was not really sexual. But, I realize he must have had some sense of what was happening. He was not afraid. I know he was trying to please me ... I used to let him drive my car. I would let him sit in my lap and drive. He had a lot of control ... I really enjoyed his company (a part from anything sexual).

"It's strange that what I did would tear me up, but a few days later it would happen again ... I would get upset and ask myself, 'How could I do that?' Sometimes, I could control it for a couple days ....

"In general, I am more drawn to children emotionally ... Sometimes, I think, 'Well, here's a parent with a wonderful kid, and they are not giving him any attention -- they are ignoring him and taking him for granted. But then, I guess that is better than abusing them like I did. I still say that I have a lot of good qualities. I used to help a lot of children. I have people who are twenty years old now who come up to me and say they remember me teaching them when they were twelve. There are a lot of positive things."

Abuse He Experienced As A Child

"When I was a boy, a nun at the school I attended told me to go home and learn how to talk. She sent me home. I never went back again. (cried) I was in the fifth grade. I had no significant father image when I was growing up. My father was fifty-four years old when I was born, so we did not do much together. I was close to my mother because she had to take me to different doctors all the time due to my birth defect. (I was the youngest child of a large family. My father is deceased now, but my mother is still alive.) I was never paddled."

Prevention Checklist For Chapter III

Some studies show that due to the reinforcing nature of deviant sexual acts, the offender may commit them again and again. The reinforcement of deviant sexual behavior comes from the thrill of secrecy or the anticipation of fantasizing about the victim or the sexual confrontation and stalking the victim.

Behavioral reinforcement results when the offender is sexually aroused by thoughts of initiating sexual acts with a child or teenager and after he has committed such acts. For the perpetrator, the physical gratification -- his feelings of power and control are not threatened by knowing he could be punished with a fine, prison and embarrassment. He is willing to take the risks because he enjoys his deviant behavior. Some researchers believe that child molesters who use a coercive and manipulative approach to victims, are reacting to anger. The molester is not able to express his frustrations, pain or anger openly and appropriately.

The offenders mentioned in this chapter were not forced or coerced into divulging their histories. I believe their attempts in relating their pasts are a positive step in rehabilitating themselves. Recovery or rehabilitation for sexual offenders involves several steps.

Offenders must admit to themselves that they offended an innocent person and that their victims were indeed victims and did not ask for the sexual advances and molestations. They must admit they need help from a counselor or therapist and then actively pursue it. It is important for offenders to develop some sort of compassion for their victims and not depend on excuses, such as, "*She wanted it or she won't remember this when she is older.*" They must acknowledge that their behavior is inappropriate, and that it must never be repeated.

Some offenders may find, in addition to counseling, that jotting thoughts down on paper about what they have done or things that happened in their pasts leading up to the molestations helps in terms of understanding themselves better. One offender I interviewed shared two poems he had written in regard to his own abuse. In one poem he titled: "*Daddy, I Love You,*" he wrote the following:

Daddy I know you love me, but how I feel the pain
Of knowing how you treated me, how you let in the rain
How you let your sense of justice and goodwill fade away
How you let your son be beaten down day by day
Daddy, I know that you meant well, that you really cared
But it was my spirit that you bared
When you turned yourself away from me
And let me be abused -- all for the sake of prosperity.
Daddy, I was so young, how was I to know
that money was your love, and I had nowhere to go
No man in my life to run and play with me
No man to teach me or give me harmony!
Daddy, I remember how you tried to show your love
How you taught me to fear in Holy God above
But fear in God soon fades into memory
As I find your angry wife abusing me!
Daddy, I love you, and I always will
With you I swallow not so bitter a pill
But I know I will never forget what you did to me
How you abandoned your duty to your own family.

This same person -- a man, who sexually offended his natural daughter, wrote yet another poem he shared with me. I believe his poetry is a direct reflection of his need and efforts to come to terms with the abuse he experienced and the abuse he imposed on a child. He wrote the following poem titled, *"Mama, I Love You."*

Mama, I know you love me, but how I feel the pain
Of knowing how you treated me, how you let in the rain;
How you let your anger rise with only me around;
And I remember how you beat me, beat me into the ground.
Mama, I know that you meant well, that you really cared;
But, it was my spirit, my soul that you bared
When you abused me when I was only a child;
And it was my life, my spirit, my soul that you defiled.
Mama, I was so young, how was I to know
That you were trying to show your love blow after blow;
And as day ended, when you kissed me goodnight,
It was your face I saw in my dreams of fright!
Mama I remember how you tried to show your love
How I prayed for understanding, and pleaded to God above
To show a little boy how to be smart, handsome and good
So that you would be pleased when you feel you should.
Mama, I love you, and I always will,
But what you forced me to swallow was indeed a bitter pill
Now I know that I might give to my children as gain
A bittersweet taste of your love, your hate, your pain!

I hope the interviews included in Chapter III of this book will help victims, offenders and society in general to understand that abuse cycles through generations, whether it be sexual, emotional or physical. I found it notable that some of the offenders I interviewed and spoke with during the process of gathering information for this book admitted they had been emotionally and/or physically abused as children, and yet the

150

abuse they involved themselves in as adults (with children) was sexual. This explains how one sort of dysfunction can spill over into dysfunctions that at face value only seem unrelated. Human beings are delicate souls -- deserving of self-respect and dignity, both of which, are stolen from victims, offenders and those immobilized by fear to take steps to avert and defend.

Checklist

___ Do not place any child or children into the trust and care of any known or suspected sex offenders even if the former offender professes to be rehabilitated.

___ Do not place any child or children into the care of any suspected or known drug or alcohol abuser.

___ Seek mental and physical advice from a licensed physician or counselor if you use and abuse controlled substances or alcohol -- particularly if you are the guardian or provider of children or if you are in the company of children.

___ Home and out-of-home environments for children should foster caring and loving atmospheres that are emotionally and physically safe.

___ If you are the parent or guardian of a child or children with special needs, thoroughly check all references and backgrounds of any person who will be assisting in child care responsibilities.

Make your concerns known up front -- that a complete background check, including possible criminal records, will be conducted, etc. This open communication to applicants may frighten off would-be offenders searching for a haven to materialize deviant thoughts or plans.

CHAPTER

"Child abuse of any kind is a terrible thing (not only in society's eyes but in the eyes of God), and sexual abuse of a child is particularly serious and devastating." Billy Graham, from column titled: *"God will care for sexually abused child."* *
{ (C) Tribune Media Services, Inc. All Rights Reserved. Reprinted with permission. }

What Are The Signs Of Sexual Abuse?

Determining Potential Dangers

Signs of sexual abuse are not always indicative of actual abuse, so it is imperative that parents, teachers, social workers, guardians or concerned others not race to conclusions. We need to play active roles in protecting children from abuse, the scars of which, can last a lifetime. We should not; however, become hysterical or unreasonable about potential dangers of such dysfunctions. We should use the information we know about emotional and physical signs to prevent confirmed and suspected cases of sexual abuse. This will stop the offender from endangering other children and from continuing to victimize the child who has decided to tell.

By making it a point to understand what potential signs are, we are empowering ourselves with knowledge, and by becoming sensitized to the rudiments of this topic, we may actually curve the number of confirmed cases of sexual abuse. Abusers rely on our ignorance. They rely on our disbelief in order to continue offending.

As the general population becomes more informed and uses the information available, offenders will be immersed with more than the fear-thrill they experience at the thought of being found out. They will be afraid of committing such acts, and hopefully a fear of real consequences will bring their shame into the limelight at more psychiatrists' and counselors' offices. This is where potential and known offenders belong; not near the bedsides, homes or in the memories of the innocent.

When dealing with a situation where a child has been allegedly molested, parents or guardians should refrain from hysterical outbursts or blaming the child. Our demeanor should be one of restraint and respect for the victim and ourselves. David Finkelhor in *SEXUALLY VICTIMIZED CHILDREN*, warns: *"minor events can balloon into major traumas"* depending upon how the child is received. * Finkelhor further reports:

... the healthiest course for many children would
be not to tell their parents. Of course, ideally
the children should tell their parents, and parents
should react in a supportive fashion. But given that
most adults in current society are likely to be shocked,
upset, and anxious, much as they might try to hide it,
it can be safely assumed that most parents are more
likely to frighten a child than comfort him or her.
Assuming such a parental reaction, proponents of this
theory would expect that on the whole children who tell
their parents should be more traumatized than those
who do not .... However, there is an alternative theory
which hypothesizes that the most traumatic thing about
such an experience is *not being able* to talk about it
(Armstrong, 1978) .... *

Not being able to talk about having been sexually victimized forces the victim into a world of secrecy -- always guarding having been victimized isolates him or her from caretakers, parents or friends who could help. When the victim or survivor has been violated by a family member, the secrecy becomes more socially intrusive. It dictates how survivors live their lives. Survivors teach themselves how to appear normal -- emotionally undistriburbed by the presence of someone who offended them. Yet, they distance themselves from any meaningful conversations about the person they know to have offended them. It is part of the way they hide what has happened to them. Initially, speaking about the abuse brings about stress and worry about whether or not the chosen confidant will be able to handle their accounts. Speaking about the abuse provides survivors with an avenue to sort things out. Parents should be very careful in how they receive information about their child having been sexually offended.

Disbelief reactions can cause children to retract or deny their first attempts at seeking protection from further abuse or comfort from past abuse. Deciding to tell for the first time can result from being unable to continue living a lie -- pretending that all is well or that the person everyone in the victim or survivor's life regards as a "dear old friend" or "special" becomes too much to bare. Part of deciding to tell comes with maturity with some survivors of sexual abuse. These survivors have spent much of their lives concealing crimes that infringed on their innocence and emotional and physical securities. This works to offenders advantages in regard to not being found out and allows them to continue offending.

For children who decide to tell, telling may be the result of being overwhelmned by an offender's requests or from the fear of being abused again overriding the fear of admitting having been sexually abused. When open communication exists between children and their caretakers, parents and/or legal guardians, children appear more esteemed and more in control -- situations potential offenders would not be as likely to venture into for fear of being caught.

For child survivors, talking about what has happened to them is a very important step to stopping further victimization. It is the step that can confirm to them that they were not at fault in any way. It is also the step that opens doors to those who feel guilty for not protecting victims or survivors. Parents, caretakers or legal guardians can use a victim or survivor's first step in changing the course of the emotional aftermath to comfort and forgive themselves as well.

Privacy and confidentiality are still important to adult and child survivors of sexual abuse. *No one wants to be labeled as the person who was sexually abused.* They want to be comforted and reassured; not held up to public scutiny or gossip.

Understanding The Worlds Of Victimized Children

Understanding how our children cope in the face of being offended makes the problem and threat of sexual abuse more real to us. It is unnerving for any of us to imagine the innocents of our human race being intruded upon and left confused and hurt. You read real accounts of former childhood victims in Chapter II, and somehow knowing that these victims survived gives us hope. We should not relax with this in our minds as a resolution.

Some survivors of sexual abuse commit suicide. A small amount are murdered by their offenders before they can even be referred to as survivors. Because the crime continues, we must do more than just survive it. We must prevent it.

We understand that getting vaccinations prevents diseases. If understanding is all we seek to do, then we are still at risk for disease. If all we do is seek an understanding of sexual abuse, and fail to use what we understand about it, then we are putting our children at risk!

Sexually offended children are forced to live with a secret. They are forced to accommodate the situation. If we continue along the same paths of indifference riddled with the occasional hysteria society has for so long traveled, we become part of the problem. We become empty armor filled with false hope for resolutions for the offended and allies for the offender.

Pieces of victims childhoods are sacrificed for obtaining even the smallest portions of normalcy. One doctor labels the accommodation as *"The Child Sexual Abuse Accommodation Syndrome." In Child Abuse & Neglect,* Vol. 7 in 1983, Roland C. Summit, Head Physician at the Community Consultation Service and Clinical Associate Professor of Psychiatry, Harbor-UCLA Medical Center in Torrance, Ca., defined and outlined this syndrome. The five categories of *The Child Sexual Abuse Accommodation Syndrome* consist of 1) Secrecy, 2) Helplessness, 3) Entrapment and accommodation; 4) Delayed, conflicted and unconvincing disclosure and 5) Retraction.

Summit explains part of the Secrecy category of the syndrome in this way:

"... secrecy is both the source of fear and the promise of safety: 'Everything will be all right if you just don't tell.' The secret takes on magical, monstrous proportions for the child. A child with no knowledge or awareness of sex and even with no pain or embarrassment from the sexual experience itself will be stigmatized with a sense of badness and danger from the pervasive secrecy .... Any attempts by the child to illuminate the secret will be countered by an adult conspiracy of silence and disbelief. 'Don't worry about things like that; that could never happen in our family.' 'Nice children don't talk about things like that.' .... The average child never asks and never tells.

"Contrary to the general expectation that the victim would normally seek help, the majority of the victims in retrospective surveys had never told anyone in their childhoods. Respondents expressed fear that they would be blamed for what had happened or that the parent would not be able to protect them from retaliation. Many of those who sought help reported that parents became hysterical or punishing or pretended that nothing had happened."*

{ Source: THE CHILD SEXUAL ABUSE ACCOMMODATION SYNDROME by Roland C. Summit, M.D. in Child Abuse & Neglect, Vol. 7., p. 181. Reprinted with permission of the author. }

Summit stated the following in his article about the Helplessness category of The Child Sexual Abuse Accommodation Syndrome when the child is fondled and touched in a sexual manner by a relative or caretaker:

" .... The normal reaction is to 'play possum,' that is to feign sleep, to shift position and to pull up the covers. Small creatures simply do not call on force to deal with overwhelming threat. When there is no place to run, they have no choice but to try to hide. Children generally learn to cope silently with terrors in the night. Bed covers take on magical powers against monsters, but they are no match for human intruders .... It is sad to hear children attacked by attorneys and discredited by juries because they claimed to be molested yet admitted they had made no protest nor outcry. The point to emphasize here is not so much the miscarriage of justice as the continuing assault on the child. If the child's testimony is rejected in court, there is more likely to be a rejection by the mother and other relatives who may be eager to restore trust in the accused adult and to brand the child as malicious ... Children are easily ashamed and intimidated both by their helplessness and by their inability to communicate their feelings to uncomprehending adults. They need an adult clinical advocate to translate the child's world into an adult-acceptable language."*

{ Source: THE CHILD SEXUAL ABUSE ACCOMMODATION SYNDROME by Roland C. Summit, M.D. in Child Abuse & Neglect, Vol. 7, p.183, 1983. Reprinted with permission of the author. }

Of the Entrapment and accommodation category of *The Child Sexual Abuse Accommodation Syndrome,* Summit wrote that the sexually abused child experiences helpless victimization.

" .... She may turn to imaginary companions for reassurance. She may develop multiple personalities, assigning helplessness and suffering to one, badness and rage to another, sexual power to another, love and compassion to another, etc. She may discover altered states of consciousness to shut off the pain or to dissociate from her body, as if looking on from a distance at the child suffering the abuse. The same mechanisms which allow psychic survival for the child become handicaps to effective psychological integration as an adult.

" .... If the child cannot create a psychic economy to reconcile the continuing outrage, the intolerance of helplessness and the increasing feelings of rage will seek active expression. For the girl this often leads to self-destruction and reinforcement of self-hate; self-mutilation, suicidal behavior ....

"For many victims of sexual abuse the rage incubates over years of facade coping and frustrating, counterfeit attempts at intimacy, only to erupt as a pattern of abuse against the offspring in the next generation .... The male victim of sexual abuse is more likely to turn his rage outward in aggressive and antisocial behavior." *
{ Source: *THE CHILD SEXUAL ABUSE ACCOMMODATION SYNDROME* by Roland C. Summit, M.D. in *Child Abuse & Neglect,* Vol. 7., p. 185, 1983. Reprinted with permission of the author. }

Of the Delayed, conflicted and unconvincing disclosure category of *The Child Sexual Abuse Accommodation Syndrome,* Summit wrote:

" .... The troubled, angry adolescent risks not only disbelief, but scapegoating, humiliation and punishment .... Not all complaining adolescents appear angry and unreliable. An alternative accommodation pattern exists in which the child succeeds in hiding any indications of conflict .... The mother typically reacts to allegations of sexual abuse with disbelief and protective denial. How could she have not known? How could the child wait so long to tell her? What kind of mother would allow such a thing to happen? .... Attorneys know that the uncorroborated testimony of a child will not convict a respectable adult. The test in criminal court requires specific proof 'beyond a reasonable doubt,' and every reasonable adult juror will have reason to doubt the child's fantastic claims. Prosecutors are reluctant to subject the child to humiliating cross-examination just as they are loath to prosecute cases they cannot win. Therefore, they typically reject the complaint on the basis of insufficient evidence. Out-of-family molesters are also effectively immune from incrimination if they have any amount of prestige. Even if several children have complained, their testimony will be impeached by trivial discrepancies in their accounts or by the countercharge that the children were willing and seductive conspirators." *

{ Source: *THE CHILD SEXUAL ABUSE ACCOMMODATION SYNDROME* by Roland C. Summit, M.D. in *Child Abuse & Neglect,* Vol. 7., pp. 186-187, 1983. Reprinted with permission of the author. }

In regard to the Retraction category of The Accommodation Syndrome, Summit wrote:

"*Whatever a child says about sexual abuse, she is likely to reverse it.* Beneath the anger of impulsive disclosure remains the ambivalence of guilt and the martyred obligation to preserve the family. In the chaotic aftermath of disclosure, the child discovers that the bedrock fears and threats underlying the secrecy are true. Her father abandons her and calls her a liar. Her mother does not believe her or decompensates into hysteria and rage. The family is fragmented ... Once again, the child bears the responsibility of either preserving or destroying the family. The role reversal continues with the 'bad' choice being to tell the truth and the 'good' choice being to capitulate and restore a lie for the sake of the family." *

{ Source: *THE CHILD SEXUAL ABUSE ACCOMMODATION SYNDROME* by Roland C. Summit, M.D. in *Child Abuse & Neglect,* Vol. 7., p. 188, 1983. Reprinted with permission of the author. }

In the first chapter of this book, I included an overall definition of sexual abuse. In this chapter, I have included some extended definitions from other researchers. Writers Eve Krupinski and Dana Weikel in *Death From Child Abuse and no one heard* define sexual abuse as including "*...any inappropriate sexual interaction with a child either physical or nonphysical and includes any attempts to exploit the child sexually.*" * **{ Source:** *Death From Child Abuse and no one heard* **by Eve Krupinski and Dana Weikel. Copyright (c) 1986 by Currier•Davis Publishing. Reprinted with permission from the publisher. }** Incest, rape and sodomy, exposing genitalia, sexual suggestions, pornography and rendering children to degrading sexual insinuations or suggestions are other forms of sexual abuse.

In face of these atrocities, children are often saturated with clues about their entrapment even when they are unable to tell. These clues are the signs we must educate and sensitize ourselves with, so that in the event our intuition beckons us to protect or to intercede, we will be able, ready and motivated with love and concern and not overwhelmed and saddled with consternation.

Not all children who are being or have been abused demonstrate the same behaviors, and many are very successful in hiding what has happened to them throughout their childhoods and lives. A vital point in understanding childhood molestation is made by Krupinski's and Weikel's research:

"Females who were abused as children are more likely to internalize their victimization by suffering from diminished self-esteem, developing passive, overly-compliant personalities, or seeking abusive spouses (modeled after their own abusers) who reinforce their already poor self-concepts. These women are often relatively unsuccessful at protecting their own children from abuse." *
{ Source: *Death From Child Abuse and no one heard* **by Eve Krupinski and Dana Weikel. Copyright (c) 1986 by Currier•Davis Publishing. Reprinted with permission from the publisher. }**

Possible Physical Signs Of Sexual Abuse In Children

1) Difficulty walking or sitting

2) Torn, stained, or bloody underclothing

3) Genital and/or anal itching, pain, swelling or burning

4) Genital and/or anal bruises or bleeding

5) Frequent urinary or yeast infections

6) Pain on urination

7) Vaginal and/or penal discharge

8) Poor sphincter control

9) Venereal disease such as gonococcal infections in the pharynx, urethra, rectum, vagina; venereal disease such as syphilis, genital herpes, trichomonas (body lice) and chlamydial infection when present beyond the first six months of life. (Chlamydia may be present at birth and remain viable for up to six months.)

10) Pregnancy

11) Frequent psychosomatic illnesses (for example, stomach aches)

12) Bruises around the mouths of infants

13) Genital lacerations

14) Vaginal and/or anal tears

15) Difficulty with urination

16) Laceration of the penis or perineum

17) Venereal sores, and/or ulcers or vaginal discharge and physical complaints with no apparent basis.

18) Thickening and/or hyperpigmentation of labial skin (especially when it resolves during out-of-home placement), horizontal diameter of vaginal opening that exceeds 4 millimeters in prepubescent girls

19) Sperm on body or clothes, sperm in the urine of a female child

20) Marked weight loss or gain.

Possible Behavioral Indicators

1) Assumes a great deal of responsibility for household chores.

2) Has vague somatic complaints such as stomachaches, headaches and/or backaches

3) Extremes in behavior, such as aggression or withdrawal

4) Poor social relations

5) Complains of soreness or moves or sits awkwardly

6) Suffers from role reversal

7) Demonstrates bizarre, sophisticated, or unusual sexual knowledge or behavior

8) Masturbates excessively

9) Suffers from "*Lolita Syndrome*" (when a younger child controls a sexual relationship with an adult)

10) Exhibits withdrawal, fantasy or infantile behavior

11) Engages in delinquent acts or runs away

12) Is not willing to change for gym class or participate in physical education

13) Sudden radical behavior change

14) Poor school performance or sudden change in grades

15) Destructive to self and/or others

16) Behaves seductively and has sexual knowledge beyond age

17) Sexually acts out or attempts to force or coerce other children to be sexual

18) Depression

19) Wears inappropriate clothing to cover the body

20) Apathetic or suicidal

21) Complaint of body odor

22) Explicit knowledge of sexual acts

23) Sexually stylized or sexualized play

24) Verbal complaints of sexual abuse

25) Expressed distortion of body image

26) Presence of intrusive or bizarre health care or health habits

27) Inappropriate absence of pain or other sensations by child

28) Regressive behavior: poor self-esteem, general feelings of guilt or shame, adolescent runaways, suicide attempts, fall in school performance or attendance, antisocial behavior, inability to trust others, pseudomature personality development.

29) Excessive cooperation or fear during genital exams

30) Sleep disturbances such as severe nightmares or problems falling asleep

31) Excessive daydreaming

32) Exhibits a positive relationship toward the offender

33) Thumb sucking

34) Talking like a baby or throwing temper tantrums

(Going back to an earlier period in life is comforting to some children. It may be a child's way of soothing themselves with feelings they received in safer environments and times.)

35) Fear of a certain environment or room, such as a bathroom, bedroom or shower, which are frequent locations of sexual abuse.

36) Failure to Thrive Syndrome: when a baby does not develop physically and mentally at a normal rate. These babies are more vulnerable to sexual abuse. Caretaker often ignores them.

37) Anger

38) Serious mental illness: There may be possible child psychoses and the development of multiple personalities as a defense mechanism.

39) Loss of appetite

40) Nightmares

41) Fear of a specific person

42) Changes in sleep patterns or problems sleeping

43) Unprovoked or unpredictable crying spells

44) Wetting the bed

45) Refusal to go to school

46) Fear of strange people or places

47) Fear of playing or sitting alone

48) Social or emotional withdrawal

49) Clinging to comforting adult figure

50) Changes in creativity

51) Taking excessive baths

52) Overly compliant behavior

53) Inappropriate sex play with peers or toys

54) Age-inappropriate understanding of sexual behavior

55) Poor peer relations or inability to make friends

56) Lack of trust towards adults or peers

57) Unable to concentrate in school

More Signs To Learn

Another sign to look for may be unexplained gifts or money possessed by the child. Children are sometimes lured into accepting bribes to "*keep the secret*" or lured into showing parts of their bodies for some kind of reward: "*Just let me look one more time,*" the offender might say. "*I promise this will be the last time.*" The offender may then give the child, for example, a bag full of candy or a treat or toy that the parent might be hesitant to purchase for the child on an everyday basis.

The offender will coerce the child to fulfill his sexual deviancies, and in turn, set the child up for what seems an inseverable thread of feeling responsible for what happened. The child does not understand the motives of the offenders -- only that it is a "*GIGANTIC SECRET.*" Victims of child sexual assault often feel, as emphasized earlier, responsible for having been preyed on. They anticipate that others unrelated to the abuse may question their motives for not telling when the abuse first occurred. If a thief broke into your home because you had faulty locks and latches, would a jury or judge hold you partially responsible for the theft? If the same thief returned again and again -- despite your efforts to keep him at bay, would you be to blame for his or her persistence? Of course, you would not be blamed. If your friend convinced you to allow him or her to copy a key to your house and later robbed you, would you be responsible for your so-called friend's actions? You would feel that you had been tricked. Admitting that you had trusted a thief would be difficult.

Behavioral symptoms of child sexual abuse may become apparent during or after the time the assaults occurred. Behaviorial symptoms may not be easily detected -- especially if the abused child is making every effort to conceal clues that he or she has been or is being offended. Behaviorial symptoms may also change after the survivors have confided the offenses or after such offenses have been discovered. It's important to remember that child behaviorial problems do *not* necessarily confirm or mean that sexual abuse has occurred. Children who have been sexually abused may demonsrate behaviorial problems or difficulties; however, not all children who demonstrate such problems have been sexually assaulted.

Still, More Signs

Seductive behavior, as mentioned earlier, is a sign that we should pay attention to. Sometimes, innocent affection and sexual activities intertwined cause a great deal of confusion and frustration in a child. A sexually abused child may learn that "*sex*" is the only way for them to receive love and acceptance. The building blocks of such dysfunctional experiences sets the child up for further sexual and emotional exploitation and victimization in adulthood.

Another sign of potential sexual abuse can be seen when a child distances him or herself from role models such as teachers. In a conversation, sexually abused children may actively avoid referring to any situation or word dealing with sex or specific body parts. Others may act indifferently toward such references. The sexually abused child may do this to keep others from suspecting that he or she feels *different* than other children his or her age.

The sexually abused child may refuse any affection such as a kiss on the cheek or a hug from a parent or fear people who are the same sex or same sex and age as his or her perpetrator (s). Abused children may discreetly avoid others in an attempt to hide the abuse. Children who have been exposed to sexual activities beyond their years often feel *different* and *isolated* from their unabused peers.

168

Other signs include sexual drawing. Sometimes, sexually abused children draw pictures -- depicting a man's penis, for instance. In addition, children who feel powerless or out of control may demonstrate over compliance with authority figures in his or her life or with peers. Susan B. Bierker in *ABOUT SEXUAL ABUSE* says:

"The children have been conditioned to be victims and have difficulty asserting themselves .... Because a victimized child feels vulnerable, powerless and unprotected, he will often withdraw from other children and adults because he has transferred the betrayal of trust caused by the offender onto others in general. Children who have maintained a trust in non-abusers may cling to others to provide what they feel is a protective shield around them. Clinging feels safe and therefore becomes exagerated. There is the fear of being alone because the protective shield is gone and the child feels very vulnerable and unable to protect himself." *
{ Source: *ABOUT SEXUAL ABUSE* **by Susan B. Bierker. Copyright (c) 1989 by Susan B. Bierker. All Rights Reserved. Reprinted with permission from the author. }**

Facts Versus Myths

The United States has a history of having more than a million children reported as abused each year. Our society is shamefully violent. *The Results of the 1996 Annual Fifty State Survey* reveals that an estimated 3,126,000 children were reported as having been maltreated in 1996.* This means that 47 children out of every 1,000 U.S. children were reported for maltreatment, and this was 6,000 more children reported than in 1995.*

Maltreatment includes sexual abuse, as well as, physical abuse, emotional maltreatment and neglect. In an article, which was published in the Aug. 9, 1985 issue of *JAMA, Journal of the American Medical Association*, sexual abuse is defined as the "*exploitation of a child for the gratification or profit of an adult... Sexual abuse may also result in physical injury or be accompanied by other signs of abuse and neglect.*" *

{ **Source:** *JAMA, Journal of the American Medical Association,* **Council on Scientific Affairs, Aug. 9, 1985, Vol. 254, No. 6, p. 798. Copyright (c) 1985. American Medical Association (AMA). Reprinted with permission of the AMA.** }

"Sexual abuse generally is perpetrated by someone known to the child and frequently continues over a prolonged period of time. Often, it does not involve sexual intercourse or physical force. The incidence is estimated at 100,000 to 250,000 cases per year; however, this type of abuse is difficult to detect and confirm." *

{ **Source:** *JAMA, Journal of the American Medical Association,* **Council on Scientific Affairs, Aug. 9, 1985, Vol. 254, No. 6, p. 798. Copyright (c) 1985. American Medical Association (AMA). Reprinted with permission of the AMA.** }

Despite such reports and a growing awareness of the problem, sexual abuse is blanketed with fears, myths and other deceptions.

Mark Everson, a North Carolina psychologist, said in an interview when I began researching and writing this book, that telling a victim, "*It is best to just forget about it*" is the wrong approach.

"*That is extremely damaging and unhealthy,*" Everson said. "*The public needs to hear that. This is not something you cover over, and keep as a family secret. Parents are not doing their children any public service by insisting that they not talk about it.*"

Everson points to another myth that said, " 'One would expect a child to tell.' Some people believe that if a child is truly innocent, then the child would have told immediately after." Everson said, drawing from a lecture given by Dr. Roland C. Summit, "We have the notion that sexual abuse is the sort of crime that can be equated to theft, for example. 'I would tell if my car stereo was stolen.' We should look at it more from the standpoint of a confession."

"This is why it is so much harder for victims to tell," said Dr. Barbara Boat, an Ohio psychologist.

"The victims of sexual abuse feel they are confessing a wrongdoing. They are faced with having to confess the things that happened to them -- the things they may feel responsible for, to their parent figures who they seek approval from," Boat said. "I think there are adults out there who still think the victim is in someway to blame. Some jurors may think this way ... There is a myth that the child should have been able to stop it (the abuse) somehow. There is the common thread of self-blame among victims," she said.

"Society kind of imposes the blame too," Everson said. "To put the blame on both evens it out (for society)," Boat said. "This is a really grassroot mentality. It seems to be the common denominator."

Another important aspect when dealing with children is to consider that all children feel omnipotent. In all innocence, children feel responsible for bad things. They feel that they are able to make things happen by thinking or wishing them into existence.

Prevention Checklist For Chapter IV

Preventing sexual abuse from ever occurring is important, but there are children who have been abused and those who will be abused due to lack of prevention education and the lack of implementing what we know about prevention.

The following checklist will be helpful in the event you suspect and/or confirm sexual abuse. It is also important in emphasizing what parents and caretakers of children must do because other prevention measures have not been used and when the cycles of abuse have been allowed to continue.

__ Familiarize yourself with the physical and emotional signs of sexual abuse listed in this chapter (e.g. fear or dislike of a particular person or place, etc.).

__ Report all suspected or witnessed cases of child abuse, whether physical, sexual or emotional to authorities in your city or community (social services, police).

__ If you suspect sexual abuse, take your child or children to a pediatrician or other medical doctor for a medical examination to check for possible venereal diseases or other injuries. Tell the physician your suspicions.

__ If you suspect sexual abuse of your own child or children, maintain a calm, nurturing and emotionally safe home environment.

__ Seek advice and guidance for your child or children and yourself from mental health clinic authorities or private psychologists, psychiatrists or counselors if you suspect sexual abuse. Have your child or children evaluated for ongoing therapy.

___ Do not expect an abused child to divulge every detail of the abuse. Believe children who claim abuse, and be prepared for possible retractions of such claims later if or when the child begins to feel guilty for telling the truth.

___ Be your child's or children's confidant. Ask questions in a calm, but concerned manner. Do not frighten the child or children with emotional outbursts, blame, disbelief, anger or punishment.

___ Prayer is always important -- especially when the innocence of children has been violated.

___ Encourage your child to talk with you by assuring him or her that telling what happened or even telling what was suggested is always the right thing to do.

Appendix For Chapter III

Many authors and researchers provide adequate definitions and distinctions between child molesters and pedophiles, but the following excerpt from *The Child Molester, An Integrated Approach to Evaluation and Treatment* by George W. Barnard, M.D., A. Kenneth Fuller, M.D., Lynn Robbins and Theodore Shaw provides helpful distinctions I hope will give more insight.

> *...pedophilia,* **which literally means** *love of children,* **is equated synonymously, but erroneously, with child sexual abuse. Whereas,** *pedophile* **and** *pedophiliac* **imply that a mental disorder is present in the individual,** *child molester* **refers to the perpetrator of a more general sexual maltreatment of children and does not connote that a mental illness exists. According to one diagnostic definition, pedophilia exists if there are "sexual deviations in which an adult engages in sexual activity with a child of the same or opposite sex." A more delineated definition specifies the following criteria:**
>
> **A. Over a period of at least six months, recurrent intense sexual urges and sexually arousing fantasies involving sexual activity with a prepubescent child or children (generally age 13 or younger).**
>
> **B. The person has acted on these urges, or is markedly distressed by them.**
>
> **C. The person is at least 16 years old and at least 5 years older than the child or children in A. ***
>
> **According to the new revision of DSM-III, a person meeting these criteria**

APPENDIX

may be considered a pedophile.
In short, pedophilia is a mental disorder that can be
subsumed under the term *child molester* --- all
pedophiles are child molesters, but not all child
molesters are diagnostically viewed as pedophiles. *
{ **Source:** *The Child Molester, An Integrated Approach to Evaluation and Treatment* **by George W. Barnard, M.D., A. Kenneth Fuller, M.D., Lynn Robbins and Theodore Shaw. Copyright (c) 1989 by Brunner/Mazel, Inc. Reprinted with permission from the publisher. }**

{ **Source:** *DIAGNOSTIC AND STATISTICAL MANUAL OF MENTAL DISORDERS REVISED, DSM-III-R.* **Copyright (c) 1987 by American Psychiatric Association. All Rights Reserved. Reprinted with permission of the publisher. }**

The Fourth Edition of the 1994 *DIAGNOSTIC AND STATISTICAL MANUAL OF MENTAL DISORDERS, DSM-IV* adds:

B. The fantasies, sexual urges, or behaviors cause
clinically significant distress or impairment in
social, occupational, or other important areas of
functioning.*
{ **Source:** *DIAGNOSTIC AND STATISTICAL MANUAL OF MENTAL DISORDERS, DSM-IV,* **Copyright (c) 1994 by American Psychiatric Association. All Rights Reserved. Reprinted with permission of the publisher. }**

It also adds that such a definition does not include an individual in late adolescence in an ongoing sexual relationship with a 12- or 13-year-old.*

Some authorities find that categorizing child sex offenders into immature, regressed and aggressive offenders, as too restrictive and not adequate to suit the varying sexual behaviors and motives of offenders. Dr. William (Bill) Tyson, a North Carolina psychologist who treats convicted sex offenders currently on probation and in group therapy, said during an interview when I began researching and writing this book that the term "pedophile" is often misunderstood and used inappropriately. "Pedophile is a real misleading term," he said.

"It needs to be closely reserved for someone who has a sexual preference for children or adolescents in a specific age range. A lot of people who get labeled as pedophiles are really not pedophiles. The true pedophile actually makes up a very small percentage of the sex offenders ... although they may be responsible for a lot more victims than the regressed molester. The 'true pedophile' is a very small component of the sex offender population." Tyson, who treats many child molesters, explains that the term pedophile places the causes for behavior in some sort of psychological functioning, "rather than where it ought to be, which is a behavioral disorder. It is a problem of impulse control and lack of control."

Tyson, who works with both victims and offenders, explains sexual offending in terms of being a behavioral problem versus a psychological one.

"Someone can have arousal to inappropriate sex partners -- but if they never act on it, it is not a problem. It may be distressing to them, but it does not make them a social problem. Where we (psychologists and therapists) get involved in having to treat and rehabilitate sex offenders is in the people who have acted on their sexual impulses.

"It is those actions that are the problem. This is a behavioral problem --- not a psychological or emotional problem. Society and the courts are not going to get upset when a person thinks dirty thoughts. It is when he or she acts on their thoughts that society and the courts get on the warpath.

"We are concerned about the actions of the people. When an offender comes to court, the classification schemes that we come up with often times attempt to psychologically or emotionally *characterize or classify people. Such attempts are relatively useless for the courts and public in understanding what the problem is. What we need are behavioral classification schemes. That is, to classify the offenders according to the types of behavior they engage in. That will often tell us more about the psychological undertones ...."*

The definition of pedophilia, Tyson explains, is construed to connoting mental illness. "*But again, if you have a pedophile who has arousal for children and a sexual preference for children, but never acts on that sexual arousal, knows it is wrong and is able to control the impulses and recognizes it as a problem, society will never know he is a pedophile. Theoretically, these people are pedophiles, but how would anybody know? ...The only way we know if a person is a pedophile is if he/she acts on their impulses or goes to a therapist and admits his thoughts or if he or she reports their thoughts to anybody ... Then, we get into the question: 'If the tree falls in the forest, does anyone hear?' If a person has arousal by or is sexually turned on by minors and never acts on it, is this person a pedophile? I can't really answer that. It is just one of those theoretical questions I prefer to leave alone,*" Tyson said.

"*What I can talk about that is meaningful and does the courts more good is to understand the type of offender in terms of behavioral characteristics of offending. I need to be able to distinguish a predator from a pedophile and a regressed offender. This does the courts a lot more good than being able to distinguish what their psychological motivation was. With the pedophile, yes, there is a psychological process of sexual preference and arousal to children. It is different from the regressed offender. But, a lot of this can be inferred from the behavior we see too.*"

Tyson, who treats mostly what he refers to as "*regressed offenders*," explains that "*predators*" or "*the morally indiscriminate offenders*" are often labeled as pedophiles by the court system and some researchers.

"*Morally indiscriminate offenders are the most dangerous,*" Tyson said. "*They need to go to prison. Predators or the morally indiscriminate --- these are the people who act out on children. They do not have a sexual preference for children. They do not form relationships. They are motivated by conquests or by their need to exploit. They are often fairly indiscriminate with who they engage in sexual relationships with.*" Tyson describes them as manipulative, cunning, head-strong and as people who set up elaborate seduction plans. He said they often masquerade as pedophiles. "*They prey on children and adolescents. In fact, when you study them closely, you find that they prey on virtually anybody they come into contact with .... I have been involved in the prosecution of a few sex offenders who fall into this category.*"

Tyson emphasizes that the predator or morally indiscriminate sex offender's goal centers around manipulation, exploitations and conquests. "*They know exactly what they are doing. Their goal in dealing with the court system and their goal in dealing with those whose goal is to lock them up is the same as their goal in the seduction and preying on their victims. That is, to prove they are smarter and better than we are and to beat the system. They will often get called or labeled pedophiles. They are not pedophiles ... Their preference is for proving that they are smarter and better and able to get away with it, and do whatever they want, and control whoever they want.*"

".... *Most predator types do not get into therapy. They avoid therapy like the plague. When they do get into therapy, they pretend to be pedophiles when they are actually not. Most of the cases with predator offenders I have been involved with have been in the process of trying to get them convicted. I have observed them as a process of testimony and investigation. Predator types are frustrating. Their belief is that what they have done is okay.*

"They consider that their job is to get you to leave them alone. They are incredibly self-righteous. They lie prolifically. They are no more frustrating than the psychopath, they just happen to be sexually offending against someone. There are some who say you can never change them. There are others who believe if you can contain them properly, you can change them."

The pedophiles, on the other hand, are motivated by what they perceive as a genuine love affair with children, Tyson explained. *"Their sexual preference is for children in much the same way we would describe somebody being heterosexual or homosexual. They tend to form long relationships until the child ages out.*

"They see them as very warm and caring relationships. They are not predatory in the same way as the morally indiscriminate. They are a very, very small part of the population and should be carefully diagnosed. The classification may be too easily viewed as an excuse."

Tyson makes another comparison. He said: *"The predator can make people feel sorry for him by putting on, 'Oh well, I just have this irresistible compulsion. I am just this sick person.' until you start finding out that they have molested a number of children of varying* ages and sexes (and others) *as well* .... *The predator or the morally indiscriminate offender does not differentiate, and may be carrying on adult relationships both hetero and homosexual simultaneously while molesting children."*

Tyson added: *"The majority of convicted sexual offenders fall into the regressed category. The regressed molester falls into the largest category. It has the most offenders in it, although it may not have the most victims. These are the poor and pitiful shmucks who are opportunistic offenders. They have deteriorated... They try to hide their involvement and mask it as caring and love and focus on the emotional content. They are immature.*

"The best classification scheme for the types of sex offenders I have seen, although it has a few limits, is Kenneth Lanning's. Lanning makes the point that attempts to try and psychologically categorize sex offenders have failed and that behavioral classifications are more useful ...."

Tyson claims that group therapy for regressed sex offenders is helpful. *"Virtually all the offenders that I see started out as victims. Society kind of takes the view that once somebody is identified as an offender, their own victimization does not matter, and this tends to be written off as an excuse.*

"I take the view that if we can correct some of the process of victimization, and identify with the person how they got to be an offender, and start by managing the behavior in question -- the antisocial behavior that has brought them into contact with the court, we can begin to make them into a person who does not offend."

180

So, how do pedophiles evolve? Some researchers believe that pedophilia is a learned behavior, *"representing early learning never replaced by later, more rewarding experiences."* *** {Source: Criminal Behavior, A Psychosocial Approach by Curt R. and Anne M. Bartol. Copyright (c) 1986 by Prentice-Hall, a Division of Simon & Schuster, Inc. Reprinted with permission of the publisher. }**

Regardless of whether pedophiles and other sorts of child molesters are the direct result of emotionally and physically unhealthy childhood environments or are results of medical *"brain"* conditions (e.g. senility,) or for whatever reason that can be sited to emphasize the realities of sexually abused children, it continues. It is fueled, as I stated in earlier chapters, through all forms of child maltreatment, drug and alcohol abuse, fictionalized television violence and sexually explicit entertainment. Responsible adults should all strive to rid our society of the problems that deprive the innocent of experiencing life as it should be for everyone.

For the concerned individual trying to understand offenders in order to prevent the victimization of our children, the bottom line is that major strides need to be made in regard to re-shaping our society -- the dysfunctional behaviors and attitudes that have placed our innocents into the accessible realm of offenders. These strides can easily be made by first understanding that dysfunctional behavior breeds more of the same, and that we have an obligation to our innocents and ourselves to protect. Acting on this obligation is more than hope for change. It is change for the better.

Childhood is the part of our lives most deserving of unconditional protection and love. Mentally stable adults are almost always the result of emotionally and physically stable childhood home environments and experiences. They are the reflections of what everyone should be. Many offenders, as I have stated earlier in this book, are the biproducts of dysfunctional family upbringings. They are the results of society's indifference and failure to intercede. They reflect mankind's failure to mend tiny holes of dysfunctional damage. A more serious and responsible approach to protecting our children against sexual assault and related abuse is the answer.

Shielding Our Innocents,

A Prevention Plan

On Child Sexual Abuse

NOTES

By Hélène Andorre Hinson Staley

Notes

My Comments To You

*North Carolina Chapter of the National Committee to Prevent Child Abuse (NCPCA), *"It shouldn't hurt to be a child"* (pamphlet), 3344 Hillsborough St., Suite 100-D, Raleigh, N.C. 27607.

*ibid.

*ibid.

*Derek Jehu, *Beyond Sexual Abuse, Therapy With Women Who Were Childhood Victims,* page 174, 1988, John Wiley & Sons, Ltd., New York, N.Y.

Chapter I: A Discussion On Prevention, Help and Forgiveness

*Colao, Flora and Tamar Hosansky. "*THE KEY TO HAVING*

FUN IS BEING SAFE, TEACHING PERSONAL SAFETY TO CHILDREN," 1982, 1983, 1987, Flora Colao, 85 Bedford Street, New York, N.Y. 10014.

*Colao and Hosansky.

*ibid.

Chapter II: Individual Recollections From Adult Survivors

(No notes on this chapter.)

Chapter III: Sex Offenders -- Who Are They?

*Ching-Tung Wang, Ph.D., Principal Researcher, Deborah Daro, D.S.W., Director. *Current Trends in Child Abuse Reporting and Fatalities: The Results of the 1996 Annual Fifty State Survey,* The National Center on Child Abuse Prevention Research, a program of The National Committee to Prevent Child Abuse, Working Paper Number 808, 332 South Michigan Avenue, Suite 1600, Chicago, Ill. 60604.

*National Committee to Prevent Child Abuse, *NCPCA Fact Sheet,* 332 South Michigan Avenue, Suite 1600, Chicago, Ill. 60604.

*Curt R. and Anne M. Bartol, *Criminal Behavior, A Psychosocial Approach,* second edition, 1986, Prentice-Hall, a Division of Simon & Schuster, Inc., Englewood Cliffs, N.J., Chapter 9, page 218.

*Bartol, et al., page 218.

*Bartol, et al., page 215.

*Idaho Department of Law Enforcement Statistical Analysis Center, *CHILD SEXUAL ABUSE IN IDAHO: THE PROBLEM, ITS IMPACT AND A PERSPECTIVE FOR CHANGE,* July, 1989, page 7-8.

*Lucy Berliner, MSW and Doris Stevens, MA, ACSW. "CLINICAL ISSUES IN CHILD SEXUAL ABUSE," *Journal of Social Work & Human Sexuality,* Vol. 1 1982/83, pages 99-100.

*Jon Conte, *A Look at Child Sexual Abuse,* 1986, *National Committee to Prevent Child Abuse,* Chicago, Ill., page 19.

*Conte, page 21.

*Conte, page 21.

Chapter IV: What Are The Signs of Sexual Abuse?

*Billy Graham, "*God will care for sexually abused child,*" The *Sanford Herald,* Sanford, N.C., September 1990.

*David Finkelhor. *SEXUALLY VICTIMIZED CHILDREN,* 1979, The Free Press, a Division of Macmillan Publishing, Co., Inc., New York, N.Y., page 106.

*Finkelhor, page 106.

*Roland C. Summit, M.D., "THE CHILD SEXUAL ABUSE ACCOMMODATION SYNDROME," Child Abuse & Neglect, Vol. 7., 1983, page 181.

*Summit, page 183.

*Summit, page 185.

*Summit, pages 186-187.

*Summit, page 188.

*Eve Krupinski and Dana Weikel, Death From Child Abuse and no one heard, 1986, Currier•Davis Publishing, Winter Park, Fla., page 101.

*Krupinski and Weikel, page 105.

*Susan B. Bierker, ABOUT SEXUAL ABUSE, 1989, Charles C Thomas Publisher, Springfield, Ill., pages 35-36.

*Ching-Tung Wang, Ph.D., Deborah Daro, D.S.W., Current Trends in Child Abuse Reporting and Fatalities: The Results of the 1996 Annual Fifty State Survey.

*ibid.

*JAMA, Journal of the American Medical Association, Council Report from the Council on Scientific Affairs, Aug. 9, 1985, Vol.

254, No. 6, page 798.

*JAMA, page 798.

Appendix For Chapter III

*George W. Barnard, M.D., A. Kenneth Fuller, M.D., Lynn Robbins and Theodore Shaw, *The Child Molester, An Integrated Approach to Evaluation and Treatment*, 1989, Brunner/Mazel, Inc., 19 Union Square, New York, N.Y., page 8.

*Barnard, et al., page 8.

*American Psychiatric Association, *DIAGNOSTIC AND STATISTICAL MANUAL OF MENTAL DISORDERS REVISED (DSM-III-R)*, Third Edition, 1987, American Psychiatric Association, Washington, D.C., page 285.

*American Psychiatric Association, *DIAGNOSTIC AND STATISTICAL MANUAL OF MENTAL DISORDERS (DSM-IV)*, Fourth Edition, 1994, American Psychiatric Association, Washington, D.C., page 528.

*American Psychiatric Association, page 528.

*Bartol, et. al., page 217.

Personal Interviews:

Dr. Barbara Walling Boat, Department of Psychiatry, University of North Carolina at Chapel Hill, interviewed Thursday, June 21, 1990 and Friday July 13, 1990.

*Boat is currently an associate professor in the Department of Psychiatry at the University of Cincinnati, Ohio. She holds a Ph.D in psychology from Case Western Reserve University in Cleveland, Ohio; a master's degree in Child Behavior and Development from the Institute of Child Behavior and Development, University of Iowa; a bachelor's degree in psychology (Summa Cum Laude) Macalester College, St. Paul, Minnesota.

Dr. Mark Douglas Everson, Department of Psychiatry, University of North Carolina at Chapel Hill, interviewed Monday, June 25, 1990 and Friday, July 13, 1990.

*Everson is a licensed practicing psychologist in North Carolina and a clinical associate professor of psychology with the Division of Child Psychiatry, Department of Psychiatry in the School of Medicine at the University of North Carolina at Chapel Hill. He holds a Ph.D in Child Development from Stanford University, Stanford, Ca. He has completed postdoctoral training in psychology with the Division for Disorders of Development and Learning at the University of North Carolina at Chapel Hill; postdoctoral training in psychology with the Infant-Parent Program, Department of Psychiatry, University of California, San Francisco, Ca.; postdoctoral training in psychology with the Child-Study Unit, Department of Pediatrics, University of California, San Francisco. He earned a bachelor's degree (Phi Beta Kappa) in psychology from Emory University in Atlanta, Ga.

Robert Hayes, private therapist, in Charlotte, N.C., interviewed September, November and December 1990.

*Hayes holds a bachelor's degree in English and Philosophy from the University of North Carolina at Charlotte and a master's degree in Human Development and Learning from the same university. Previous positions include working as a family therapist and counseling patients at Mecklenburg County Mental Health Center. Hayes provides therapy for many people, including victims of sexual, emotional and physical abuse. He also works with people who have been diagnosed with Multiple Personality Disorder (MPD) -- currently called Dissociative Identity Disorder (DID).

Father Craig Lister, Episcopal priest, Saint Dunstan's Episcopal Church, Carmel Valley, Ca. (Interviewed in October 1990 in Sanford, N.C.)

*Lister holds a bachelor's degree in American history from Amherst College, Amherst, Mass. He holds a master's of divinity from Episcopal Divinity School in Cambridge, Mass. His special area of competence at this school was Biblical Studies. Other aspects of his education include working as a chaplain at Children's Hospital in Boston, Mass. and at Peter Bent Brigham Hospital in Boston, Mass. He was ordained as a deacon in July 1978 and as a priest in December 1978. Past positions include working as a youth minister, curate, assistant rector and rector of various churches.

Rev. Charles Steven Rosser, minister of Abundant Life Christian Center, Spring Lane, Sanford, N.C., interviewed Thursday, July 12, 1990.

*Rosser holds a bachelor's degree in Biblical literature from Southeastern College in Lakeland, Fla. and an associate's degree in broadcasting (RTV) from Central Carolina Community College in Sanford, N.C. He worked as an associate pastor of Abundant Life Christian Center for one year in 1984, and has, since then, been the minister of Abundant Life.

*Dr. Roland C. Summit has spent over 28 years as a community psychiatrist, with the past 24 years devoted almost exclusively to child abuse consultation. He is a founding member of the Parents Anonymous Board of Directors and a founder of the Los Angeles County Child Sexual Abuse Project and the UCLA Family Support Program. His writings span the modern emergence of sexual abuse awareness, from *Sexual Abuse of Children: A Clinical Spectrum* in 1978, through the pivotal *Child Sexual Abuse Accommodation Syndrome* (1983), to *The Dark Tunnels of McMartin* in 1994. He has lectured throughout the United States and Canada, keynoting conferences also in Australia, England and Sweden. Dr. Summit serves as a consultant to entertainment and news media, to state legislators and to federal agencies concerned with issues of victimization. He has been honored with several awards, including the California Governor's Pioneer Award and the Kempe National Center's Brandt F. Steele Award for outstanding contributions in the field of Child Abuse and Neglect. Dr. Summit is a graduate of the School of Medicine, University of California, Los Angeles. He also holds a bachelor's degree from Pomona College, Claremont, Ca.

Dr. William (Bill) Tyson, psychologist, in Charlotte, N.C., interviewed Friday, Sept. 21, 1990 and Friday, Sept. 28, 1990 and in October, November, December 1990.

*Tyson is in the private practice of Clinical and Forensic Psychology. He is known in North Carolina for his work and has consulted, testified and submitted evaluations to State, Federal and Military Courts in approximately 1,500 proceedings. He holds a Ph.D in clinical psychology from the University of Massachusetts, Amherst; a master's degree in clinical psychology from the University of Massachusetts, Amherst; a bachelor's degree in psychology (honors/Summa Cum Laude) from Temple University in Philadelphia. He is licensed by the North Carolina Psychology Board.

190

Shielding Our Innocents,

A Prevention Plan

On Child Sexual Abuse

REFERENCES

By Hélène Andorre Hinson Staley

References

Abel, Gene G., M.D.; Judith V. Becker, Ph.D; Jerry Cunningham-Rathner, BA; Mary Mittelman, DrPH; and Joanne L. Rouleau, Ph.D; *"Multiple Paraphiliac Diagnoses among Sex Offenders,"* Bulletin of the American Academy of Psychiatry and the Law, Vol. 16, No. 2, pps. 153-168., 1988.

Abel, Gene G., M.D., Judith V. Becker, Mary Mittelman, Jerry Cunningham-Rathner, Joanne L. Rouleau and William D. Murphy, *"Self-Reported Sex Crimes of Nonincarcerated Paraphiliacs,"* JOURNAL OF INTERPERSONAL VIOLENCE, Vol. 2, No. 1, pps. 3-25, March 1987.

Adams, Caren and Jennifer Fay, *NO MORE SECRETS, protecting your child from sexual assault,* 1981, Impact Publishers, Post Office Box 1094, San Luis Obispo, Ca. 93406.

American Psychiatric Association. *DIAGNOSTIC AND STATISTICAL MANUAL OF MENTAL DISORDERS,* Fourth Edition, (DSM-IV), 1994, American Psychiatric Association, Washington, D.C.

American Psychiatric Association. *DIAGNOSTIC AND STATISTICAL MANUAL OF MENTAL DISORDERS*

REVISED, (DSM-III-R), 1987, American Psychiatric Association, Washington, D.C.

Armstrong, Louise. *Kiss Daddy Goodnight*, 1978, Pocket Books, a Division of Simon & Schuster, Inc., 1230 Avenue of the Americas, New York, N.Y. 10020.

Barnard, George W., M.D., A. Kenneth Fuller, M.D, Lynn Robbins and Theodore Shaw. *The Child Molester, An Integrated Approach to Evaluation and Treatment*, 1989, Brunner/Mazel, Inc. 19 Union Square, New York, N.Y. 10003, page 8.

Bartol, Curt R. and Anne M. Bartol. *Criminal Behavior, A Psychosocial Approach,* second edition, 1986, Prentice-Hall, a Division of Simon & Schuster, Inc., Englewood Cliffs, N.J. 07632, pages 201-218.

Beogehold, Betty. *It's Okay to Say "Don't!", A Book About Protecting Yourself,* A Golden Book, 1985, New York, Western Publishing Company, Inc., Racine, Wis. 53404.

Berry, Joy. *LET'S TALK SERIES: FEELING ANGRY, FEELING AFRAID, SAYING NO, FEELING SAD, BEING HELPFUL and NEEDING ATTENTION,* 1996, Scholastic Inc., 555 Broadway, New York, N.Y. 10012.

Bierker, Susan B., M.S.W., A.C.S.W., *ABOUT SEXUAL ABUSE,* 1989, Charles C. Thomas Publisher, 2600 South First Street, Springfield, Ill. 62794-9265, pps. 25, 35-36, 187, 204.

Bradshaw, John. *HOMECOMING, Reclaiming and Championing Your Inner Child,* 1990, Bantam Books, a Division of Bantam Doubleday Dell Publishing Group, Inc., 1540 Broadway, New York, N.Y. 10036.

Briggs, Dorothy Corkille. YOUR CHILD'S SELF-ESTEEM, 1970, Doubleday, a Division of Bantam Doubleday Dell Publishing Group, Inc., 1540 Broadway, New York, N.Y. 10036.

Colao, Flora and Tamar Hosansky. "THE KEY TO HAVING FUN IS BEING SAFE, TEACHING PERSONAL SAFETY TO CHILDREN." 1982, 1983, 1987, 85 Bedford St., New York, N.Y. 10014.

Conte, Jon, A Look at Child Sexual Abuse, 1986, National Committee for Prevention of Child Abuse, Chicago, Ill., page 19-21.

Finkelhor, David. SEXUALLY VICTIMIZED CHILDREN. 1979, The Free Press, a Division of Macmillan Publishers Co., Inc., New York and Collier Macmillan Publishers, London, 106.

Freeman, Eileen Elias. Angelic Healing, Working with Your Angels to Heal Your Life, 1994, Warner Books, Inc., 1271 Avenue of the Americas, New York, N.Y. 10020.

Freeman, Lory. LOVING TOUCHES, A BOOK FOR CHILDREN ABOUT POSITIVE, CARING KINDS OF TOUCHING, 1986, Parenting Press, Inc. Post Office Box 75267, Seattle, WA. 98125.

Gebhard, Paul H., John H. Gagnon, Wardell B. Pomeroy, Cornelia V. Christenson. Sex Offenders, An Analysis of Types, 1965, Harper and Row Publishers, and Paul B. Hoeber, Inc., Medical Books, New York.

Girard, Linda Walvoord. MY BODY IS PRIVATE, 1984, Albert Whitman & Company, 6340 Oakton St., Morton Grove, Ill. 60053.

Graham, Billy. "*God will care for sexually abused child*," Sept. 12, 1990, *The Sanford Herald,* Sanford, N.C. 27330.

Hinson-Staley, Helene Andorre. "*What we can do to prevent child abuse*," Tuesday, March 14, 1995, Community News, *The Raleigh News and Observer,* Raleigh, N.C.

Hinson, Helene. "*Children in court, steps being taken to make their giving testimony less traumatic*," June 6, 1987; "*Sanford man found innocent*," Oct. 15, 1986; "*Defendant acquitted of rape charge*," May 20, 1987; "*Testimony continues in case*," Dec. 3, 1986; "*Jury is deliberating fate of defendant in rape case*," Dec. 5, 1986; "*Trial moves into third day*," Dec. 4, 1986; "*Jury deadlocks in rape case*," Dec. 6, 1986; "*Sanford youth pleads guilty to lesser charge*," May 21, 1987; "*Sanford man handed 30-year prison term*," Oct. 14, 1986; "*Jury Duty, Former jurors recount their thoughts, while serving in court in Lee County*," Feb. 23, 1987; "*What, exactly is truth?*" Dec.31, 1987; *The Sanford Herald,* Sanford, N.C. 27330.

Hinson, Helene. "*Convicted killer sentenced to die*," April 29, 1988; "*Facing death sentence, McCarver finds God*," April 28, 1988; "*Lee McCarver says absent parents, no guidance are to blame for his brothers act of violence*," May 1, 1988; "*Girl testifies man forced her to have sex*," June 28, 1988; "*Man given six years in indecent liberties case*," June 30, 1988; "*Guardians program represents abused neglected children*," March 6, 1988; "*Council seeks to assist abused, neglected children*," March 10, 1988; *The Concord Tribune,* Concord, N.C.

Idaho Department of Law Enforcement Statistical Analysis Center, *CHILD SEXUAL ABUSE IN IDAHO: THE PROBLEM, ITS IMPACT AND A PERSPECTIVE FOR CHANGE*, July, 1989, pps. 8, 10.

Jehu, Derek in association with Marjorie Gazan and Carole Klassen. *Beyond Sexual Abuse, Therapy With Women Who Were Childhood Victims*, 1988, John Wiley & Sons, Ltd., New York, pps. 174-175.

JAMA, Journal of the American Medical Association, "AMA *Diagnostic and Treatment Guidelines Concerning Child Abuse and Neglect*," Council Report from the Council on Scientific Affairs, Aug. 9, 1985, Vol. 254, No. 6, pps. 796-800.

Journal of Social Work & Human Sexuality, "CLINICAL ISSUES IN CHILD SEXUAL ABUSE, by Lucy Berliner, MSW and Doris Stevens, MA., ACSW, Vol. 1, 1982/83, The Haworth Press, Inc., New York, N.Y. pps. 93-107.

Krupinski, Eve and Dana Weikel. *Death From Child Abuse and no one heard*, 1986, Currier•Davis Publishing, Winter Park, Fla., pps. 101, 105.

Lerner, Ph.D, Harriet G. *The Dance of ANGER, A WOMAN'S GUIDE TO CHANGING PATTERNS OF INTIMATE RELATIONSHIPS*, 1985, Harper and Row Publishers, Inc., 10 East 53rd Street, New York, N.Y. 10022.

Manshel, Lisa. *Nap Time, The True-Story of Sexual Abuse at a Suburban Day-Care Center*, 1990, Kensington Publishing Corp., 475 Park Avenue South, New York, N.Y. 10016.

Mayer, Mercer and Gina Mayer. *JUST LOST*, A Golden Book, 1994, Western Publishing Company, Inc., Racine, Wis., 53404.

Mayer, Mercer. *I WAS SO MAD* and *ALL BY MYSELF*, A Golden Book 1983, Western Publishing Company, Inc., Racine, Wis., 53404.

Morris, Michelle. *If I Should Die Before I Wake*, 1982, J.P. Tarcher, Inc., 9110 Sunset Blvd., Los Angeles, Ca. 90069.

North Carolina Chapter of the National Committee to Prevent Child Abuse, 3344 Hillsborough St., Suite 100-D, Raleigh, N.C. 27607.

Russell, Diana E.H. *THE SECRET TRAUMA, Incest in the Lives of Girls and Women,* 1986, Basic Books, Inc. Publishers, New York.

The Sanford Herald, Sanford, N.C., *"Suspect claims he molested 1,000,"* Sept. 20, 1990, page 2A.

Spira, James L. *Treating Dissociative Identity Disorder,* 1996, Jossey-Bass, Inc. Publishers, 350 Sansome Street, San Francisco, Ca.

Spock, M.D., Benjamin and Michael B. Rothenberg, M.D., *Dr. Spock's Baby and Child Care,* 1985, E.P. Dutton, a Division of Penguin Books, USA, Inc., 2 Park Avenue, New York, N.Y. 10016.

196

Summit, M.D., Roland C., "*THE CHILD SEXUAL ABUSE ACCOMMODATION SYNDROME*," *Child Abuse & Neglect*, Vol. 7., 1983, page 177-195.

Wagner, Jan. *RAISING SAFE KIDS IN AN UNSAFE WORLD, 30 Simple Ways to Prevent Your Child From Becoming Lost, Abducted, or Abused*, 1996, Avon Books, a Division of The Hearst Corporation, 1350 Avenue of the Americas, New York, N.Y. 10019.

Wagner, Jan. *NOT MY CHILD!*, 1994-95, Yellow Dyno Publishing, 7101 Highway 71 West, Suite A-9, Austin, Tx. 78735.

Wang, Ph.D., Ching-Tung and Deborah Daro, D.S.W. *Current Trends in Child Abuse Reporting and Fatalities: The Results of the 1996 Annual Fifty State Survey*, prepared by The National Center on Child Abuse Prevention Research, a program of The National Committee to Prevent Child Abuse, Working Paper Number 808, 332 South Michigan Avenue, Suite 1600, Chicago, Ill. 60604.

Youngs, Ph.D, Ed.D, Bettie B. *How to Develop Self-Esteem In Your Child, 6 Vital Ingredients*, 1991, A Fawcett Columbine Book, Published by Ballatine Books, a Division of Random House, Inc., New York.

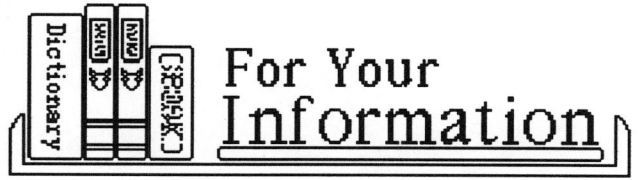

For Your
Information

FEDERAL LAWS

General statutes vary from one state to the next; however, I have decided to cite a few interesting sections of federal law as of 1994 that you can look up in *Title 18 -- Crimes and Criminal Procedure, Chapter 109A -- Sexual Abuse,* and *Chapter 110 -- Sexual Exploitation And Other Abuse Of Children,* pps. 406-414.

If you would like to read what your state laws are in regard to sexual abuse, contact your local state law library or law school or university library or ask an attorney.

If you are interested in finding out what the actual federal statutes say, consider reading sections:

2241. Aggravated sexual abuse

2242. Sexual abuse

2243. Sexual abuse of a minor or ward

2244. Abusive sexual contact

2245. Sexual abuse resulting in death

2247. Repeat offenders

2251. Sexual exploitation of children

2251A. Selling or buying children

2252. Certain activities relating to material involving the sexual exploitation of minors.

*Note:

All data gathered from personal interviews with adult survivors and perpetrators was done on a volunteer basis for the purpose of comforting victims and survivors and for inspiring and encouraging prevention. Names were withheld to protect the identities of survivors and offenders.

Graphic Artist / Cover Designer: Michael Philbeck, The Touchberry Group, Inc.